# Knitting School

A Complete Course

Sterling Publishing Co., Inc.
New York

# contents

Translated by Kelly Ramke and Maria Elena Sandovici.

**Library of Congress Cataloging-in-Publication Data**

[Scuola di maglia. English]
Knitting school / [English translation by Sterling Publishing
Company].
    p. cm.
    Originally published in 1990 in Italy by Fabbri editori.
    Includes index.
    ISBN 1-4027-0519-0
    1. Knitting. I. Sterling Publishing Company. II. Fabbri edi-
tori.
TT820.S43513 2003
746.43'2-dc21
                        2003005724

10 9 8 7 6 5 4 3

Published by Sterling Publishing Co., Inc.
387 Park Avenue South, New York, NY 10016
Originally published in Italy by Fabbri Editorial Group under the title
*Scuola di Maglia*
© 1990 by Fabbri Editorial Group, Bompiani, Sonzogno, Etas SpA,
Milano
English translation © 2003 by Sterling Publishing Co., Inc.
Distributed in Canada by Sterling Publishing
℅ Canadian Manda Group, One Atlantic Avenue, Suite 105
Toronto, Ontario, Canada M6K 3E7
Distributed in Great Britain by Chrysalis Books Group PLC,
The Chrysalis Building, Bramley Road, London W10 6SP, England.
Distributed in Australia by Capricorn Link (Australia) Pty. Ltd.
P.O. Box 704, Windsor, NSW 2756, Australia
*Manufactured in China*
*All rights reserved*

Sterling ISBN 1-4027-0519-0

# before getting started

**K**nitting is easy, relaxing, and fun. You do not need many tools to start.

## ■ what to use

**The Needles** are the basic instruments in knitting. They can be made from metal, plastic, or wood. They come with a single point (for executing all the flat surfaces), or with a double point (usually in a set of four or five called a double-pointed needle set for knitting articles, such as socks, in a circular manner), or circular (made from two needle points joined by a flexible strand for knitting an article without having to seam pieces together). All needles are available in different sizes, from very small to very large ones. The thicker the yarn, the larger the needles generally need to be. It is also very useful to have a cable needle (a small needle that is usually slightly bent in the middle) handy to use when setting aside part of your work, such as, when you knit cable pattern stitches.

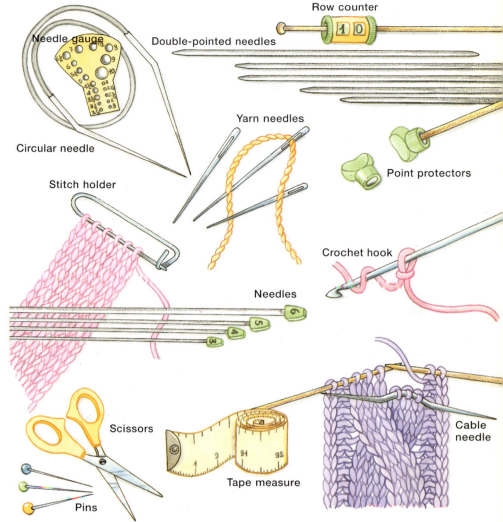

Row counter · Double-pointed needles · Needle gauge · Yarn needles · Point protectors · Stitch holder · Crochet hook · Needles · Scissors · Tape measure · Cable needle · Pins · Circular needle

---

### How to Knit a Gauge Sample (or Swatch)

Making a gauge sample, and using the same needles, yarn, and pattern as for the planned project, is an important first step of any knitting job. Usually the swatch should be about a 5-inch (12-cm) square. Lay the finished swatch flat without stretching it, measure 3 inches (8 cm) in width, then in length, and count how many stitches across and how many rows in length it corresponds to. If this count does not match that given in the instructions, you need to try again using larger or smaller needles until you get the required number of rows and stitches. Knitting to the specified gauge is essential for your project to match the pattern's size. If you alter the directions, the gauge gives the number of stitches or rows to change per inch you wish to add or subtract.

**The stitch holder** is like a large safety pin that is used to hold those stitches not being worked on out of the way without their becoming undone.

**The row counter** is inserted on the needle and increased row by row as you knit, allowing you to keep track of how many rows you have done.

**The needle gauge** is useful for determining the size of the needles that do not have a number imprinted on them (for example, double-pointed needles).

**The yarn needle with blunt tip** is useful for finishing touches, such as sewing seams, weaving in yarn ends, and embroidered designs.

Other useful accessories include **markers**, a **crochet hook**, a **tape measure**, **scissors**, and **pins**.

3

Shoulder · Neck · Shoulder · Length of Sleeve · Shoulder · Total Width · Total Length · Length of Underarm · Wrist · Width of Edge

Example of adapting the pattern: the base (in solid black line), the mirror image (in dotted line), the changes (in red).

FRONT · SLEEVE · BACK

## ■ designing your own sweater

After you have completed several knitted garments following the patterns, you may be ready to try making one of your own design, or to adapt the pattern in some special way. This book presents a variety of neck openings, sleeve treatments, tailoring finishes, and final decorations to help you create a garment that is unique and well constructed.

Some basic how-to information is presented throughout the book. There are also many new or different techniques that you may want to practice and incorporate into your design. If there are references to special

methods (e.g., a special way to bind off) that you are unfamiliar with, check the table of contents and index to find out where they are presented in the book so you can practice them.

To plan your own garment, you need to know the size and shape of the pieces you will be knitting and the gauge for yarn and needles you plan to use. Start with a simple shape (see diagrams above) and determine the measurements needed to fit. Measuring one of your own garments can help. Make a cardboard pattern for each piece you want to knit and use it as a guide when

you work so you can knit to proper shape, increasing or decreasing as needed.

Make a gauge sample for the yarn you plan to use and determine how many stitches per inch/cm. Measure your pattern at the lower edge and multiply gauge (e.g., 5 stitches per inch) and number of inches across (e.g., 12 inches); the resulting number, 60 in this case, is how many stitches to cast on. Measure the pattern at several places to figure the number of increases needed and where they have to be worked. Be sure to recheck your math carefully

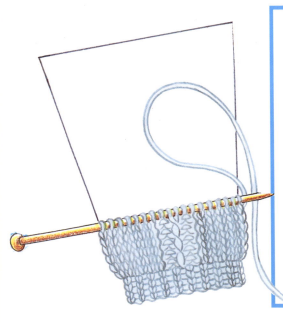

## Dictionary of Abbreviations and Terms

**beg:** beginning

**dc:** double crochet

**dec:** decrease stitch

**dp:** double pointed

**k:** knit

**k2tog:** knit 2 stitches together as one

**inc:** increase

**lp:** loop

**p:** purl

**p2tog:** purl 2 stitches together as one

**psso:** pass slip stitch over

**rnd:** round (circular row)

**rnds:** rounds

**sc:** single crochet

**sl:** slip

**sl st:** slip stitch

**st:** stitch

**sts:** stitches

**tog:** together

**yo:** yarn over

**place marker on needle:** put a ring or loop of colored yarn on needle to separate stitches

**place marker in work:** use a safety pin or tie on strand of colored yarn to mark a stitch or row

**turn work:** turn piece around so back of work on previous row is now toward you

**work even:** work without decreasing or increasing

**\* . . . \*:** repeat material between asterisks

# the yarn

Yarn and craft stores offer an extraordinary variety of yarns with very different characteristics. In order to make the right choice, consider the style of the sweater you wish to knit and the purpose it will serve so that you can find the most suitable yarn.

Yarn is made by spinning together strands of natural fibers (animal and plant) or chemical fibers (synthetic) or a blend of both natural and synthetic fibers.

Wool was once the most commonly encountered yarn in knitting. Some of the best known wools are merinos, Shetland, and lambswool; some of the most prized wools are cashmere, mohair, angora, vicuña, alpaca, and camel hair. Another natural animal fiber is silk, made by the cocoons of silkworms in the form of silk floss which is then treated. Among natural plant fibers, there are cotton, linen, hemp, and jute, even though the latter is rarely used.

Chemical fibers are obtained through transforming a natural substance, cellulose, (orlon, dralon, leacryl) and synthetic fibers, obtained from petroleum derivatives (acrylics, polyamid, polyesters).

Many present-day combinations of natural and chemical fibers can render yarn more elastic, imaginative, and versatile, and even more economical and easy to care for.

Depending on the spinning method used, yarn can be softer, more or less twisted, curled, and of different thickness and weight. Also, yarn can differ in strength and consistency, depending on the number of threads or plies that are spun into one. A ply is a name that is given to each particular yarn (for instance, knitting worsted is a 4-ply yarn and other yarns may be 2 or 3-ply yarns). This number indicates the strength of the yarn but never its thickness because the plies can be of various diameters. Finally, among the most appreciated qualities of yarn is its elasticity. If a yarn regains its original measurements after being stretched, this can be a guarantee that once you knit it into a sweater it will maintain its shape.

There are many types of yarn on the market, which vary according to their content, structure, quality, and use. The following page indicates the characteristics and uses of the best known types of yarn. The needles appropriate for knitting each type are usually indicated on the label of each ball of yarn.

# the yarn

### SHETLAND
**Description:** wool of the Shetland sheep
**Weight:** light
**Usage:** sports garments

### SPORT
**Description:** pure or mixed wool
**Weight:** light
**Usage:** sweaters, scarves, stockings, gloves, hats

### MOHAIR
**Description:** hair of Angora goats, usually mixed with other fibers
**Weight:** extremely light
**Usage:** warm but light garments, shawls

### KNITTING WORSTED
**Description:** pure or mixed fibers, 4 ply
**Weight:** medium
**Usage:** sweaters, heavy jackets

### CABLE
**Description:** pure or mixed wool
**Weight:** medium
**Usage:** sweaters, suits, jackets

### ALPACA
**Description:** wool of the alpaca, soft and vaporous
**Weight:** light
**Usage:** sweaters and expensive shawls

### CHENILLE
**Description:** yarn made of cotton or synthetic fabrics with short and interlaced tufts
**Weight:** from light to heavy
**Usage:** sweaters, jackets, trimmings, shawls, hats

### BABY
**Description:** wool or synthetic
**Weight:** extremely light
**Usage:** garments for newborns

### LAMÉ
**Description:** multicolored yarn, made out of metal yarn mixed with other fibers
**Weight:** extremely light
**Usage:** elegant garments, shawls

### BOUCLÉ
**Description:** multicolored yarn, with curled yarns
**Weight:** from light to heavy
**Usage:** sweaters, garments, jackets

### COTTON
**Description:** less elastic than wool
**Weight:** from light to heavy
**Usage:** sweaters, collars, elegant garments, sports clothes

# casting on

There are many ways to cast on stitches to form the foundation row. Here are several of the more common ways to cast stitches onto the knitting needles. Three methods are presented: starting with one needle, with two pieces of yarn, or with two needles.

**1** Wrap the yarn from under your left thumb as shown, then up and around your left index finger, forming a ring.

**2** With the tip of the right-hand needle, draw the yarn as shown from the underside of the ring that you have formed.

## ■ casting on with one needle

Leaving a long end about three times the desired length of the starting edge, hold the yarn in your left hand and a needle in your right hand.

**3** With your right hand, wrap the yarn (stemming from the ball of yarn) under the needle tip, then up and over the needle to the right as shown.

**4** With the left index finger, slip the ring over the tip of the needle.

**5** Remove index finger and pull yarn to tighten knot below first stitch. Repeat to form stitches for starting edge.

# casting on

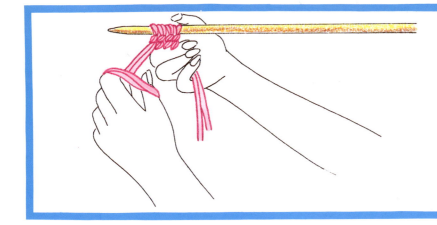

## Casting On with Two Pieces of Yarn

Use this type of casting on when you need a very firm edge, even if it is not elastic. Follow the same steps as when casting on with one needle but use a doubled strand of yarn.

## ■ casting on with two needles

This method is useful for adding new stitches to a work already in progress. Form first stitch as shown on previous page, then pass the needle to left hand and hold second needle in right hand.

**1** Insert tip of right-hand needle into front loop of the stitch just made, as shown, and wrap yarn (from ball) around right needle tip from the back, up and over the needle to right.

**2** Withdraw right-hand needle a little to pull second stitch forward.

**3** Slip second stitch onto left-hand needle, in front of the first.
Continue step 1 until you have added all the stitches needed to the left-hand needle.

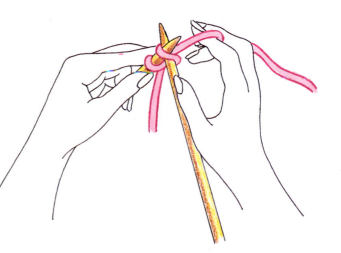

# knitting and purling

**A**fter having cast on the stitches, the first thing you need to do is learn how to knit and purl. These are the basic stitches in knitting.

## ■ the knit stitch (k)

**1** Hold the needle with the stitches in your left hand, supporting it with the little finger and guiding it with the ring and middle fingers. Keep thumb lightly pressing on needle, guiding stitches to tip with index finger.

**2** Wrap the yarn from the ball around the little finger of right hand, as shown, pass it over ring finger, under middle finger and over index finger.

**3** Pick up right-hand needle. As you knit, guiding with thumb, insert the needle tip into stitches on left-hand needle while index finger directs the movement of yarn.

**4** Keeping the yarn you are working with behind needle, insert right-hand needle (from front to back) in front loop of first stitch on left-hand needle.

**5** With right index finger, wrap yarn from back to front, then up and over right-hand needle, then back down behind same needle.

**6** Withdraw right-hand needle a little to pull new stitch forward, letting this new stitch slip onto right-hand needle and dropping old stitch off left-hand needle. Continue working each stitch across, passing new stitches to right needle and sliding old stitches off left needle.
　　If you turn work around at the end of each row and keep knitting rows, you will form a basic pattern called **garter stitch**, which looks like a series of horizontal ridges.

# knitting and purling

## ■ the purl stitch (p)

**1** Turn work so that the back of knitted stitches is toward you. Hold needle with stitches in left hand. Insert right-hand needle into front loop of first stitch of left needle, from right to left. Yarn is at front of work.

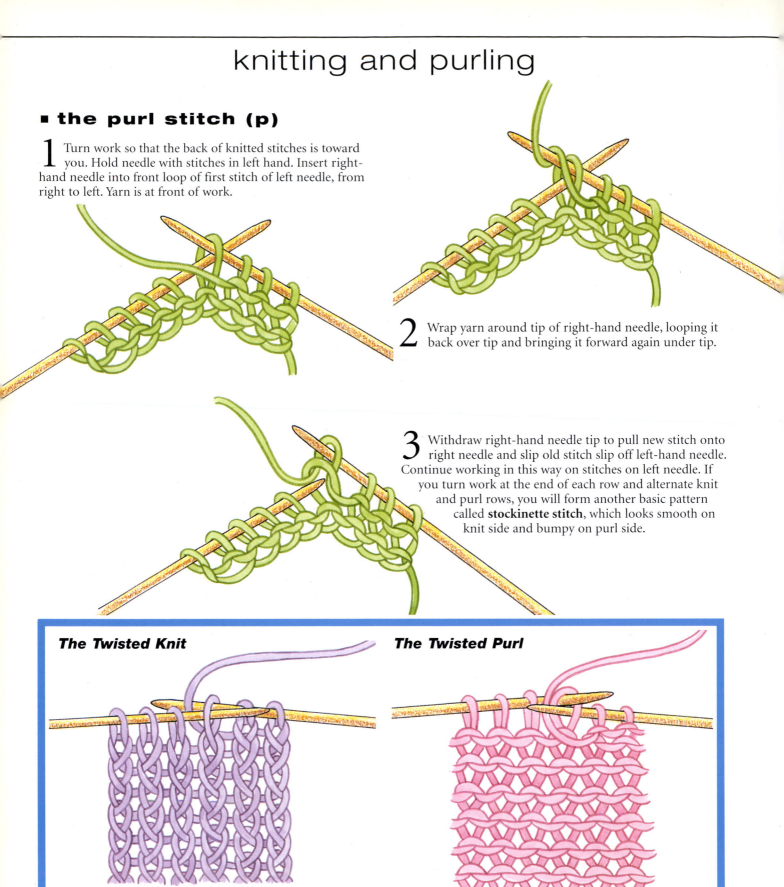

**2** Wrap yarn around tip of right-hand needle, looping it back over tip and bringing it forward again under tip.

**3** Withdraw right-hand needle tip to pull new stitch onto right needle and slip old stitch slip off left-hand needle. Continue working in this way on stitches on left needle. If you turn work at the end of each row and alternate knit and purl rows, you will form another basic pattern called **stockinette stitch**, which looks smooth on knit side and bumpy on purl side.

### The Twisted Knit

Work as for regular knit stitch, but insert right needle through back loop of the stitch. The twisted stitches are less elastic and, therefore, your garment will not easily lose its shape.

### The Twisted Purl

Work as if doing a normal purl but wrap yarn under needle, then up over the needle. It is useful to know a twisted purl stitch, although it is used less often than twisted knit.

# slip stitch and passing slip stitch over

There are several ways to vary the basic knit and purl stitches for decorative purposes. These variations include slip stitch, passing slipped stitch over, yarn over, long stitch, and crossed stitch.

## Pass Slip Stitch Over (psso)

This variation of knit and purl slipped stitches is used to decrease number of stitches.

The method may differ from slip stitches above in how stitch is slipped onto right needle. When you knit, your yarn stays in back of the work; when you purl, it stays in front.

**1** **Pass slip stitch over single stitch.** Slip a stitch without knitting it from left to right needle (slip as if to purl, as shown, for a twisted stitch, or as if to knit for a flat stitch). Knit next stitch, and with left needle, draw slipped stitch over stitch just knitted and drop it (1 stitch is decreased).

**2** **Pass slip stitch over double stitch.** Pass a slip stitch as if to knit from left to right needle. Insert right needle through 2 stitches on left needle and knit them as if 1 stitch. Then, with left needle, draw slipped stitch over double stitch and drop it (2 stitches decreased).

## ▪ slip stitch (sl st)

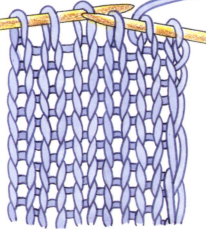

**1** **Slip stitch on knit rows.** Yarn stays in back of work. Insert right needle as if to purl (right to left) through stitch on left needle and slip it onto right needle without working it. (It will then be in the correct position when you work it on the next row.)

**2** **Slip stitch on purl rows.** Yarn stays in front of work. Slip stitch onto right needle without purling it.

# yarn over

## ■ yarn over (yo)

This stitch is used in lace patterns or to increase number of stitches by adding a loop that is worked as a stitch on next row. The loop makes a hole or eyelet in work.

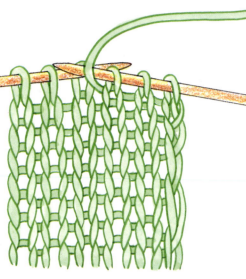

**1** **Yarn over in knit.** Bring yarn from back to front of work under needle, then wrap it over the right needle; with yarn now in back, continue to knit across row. On next row, work loop as a stitch (purl on purl row, knit on knit row).

**2** **Yarn over in purl.** Start with yarn in front, wrap it up over left needle and bring it back to front under needle tip; continue to purl across row. On next row, work loop as a stitch.

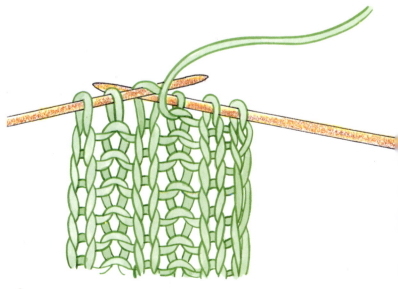

**3** **Yarn over between knit and purl.** After knitting stitch, bring yarn to front of work, then wrap it over right needle and bring it forward again to purl next stitch.

**4** **Yarn over between purl and knit.** After purling stitch, leave yarn in front and knit next stitch. (Yarn will automatically wrap over needle to back and form yarn over.)

# long stitch and crossed stitch

## ■ long stitch

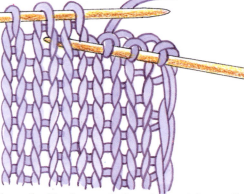

**1** Long stitch worked in the row below. Insert right needle through center of stitch just below next stitch on left needle. Wrap yarn around tip of right needle to knit and draw new stitch through on right needle, sliding unworked stitch and one below it (just worked) off left needle. Unworked stitch will undo itself but be caught on long stitch.

**2** Long stitch worked several rows below. This is used for honeycomb pattern. Work 4 rows in stockinette stitch (knit 1 row, purl 1 row) before establishing pattern. Work a long stitch 3 rows (or as directions indicate) below next stitch on left needle. Draw new stitch through, sliding unworked stitch off left needle and undoing stitches below it back to new long stitch.

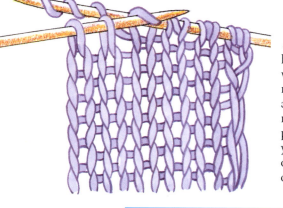

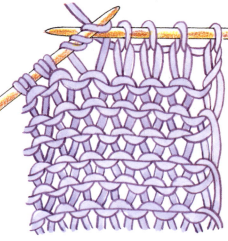

**3** Long stitch formed with yarn over. This is used in loose-knit patterns. Knit, wrapping yarn around right needle 3 times (or more times, as directed) for each stitch. On next row, work stitches (knit or purl, as directed), using only 1 yarn-over loop for each original stitch, sliding off others to form long stitch.

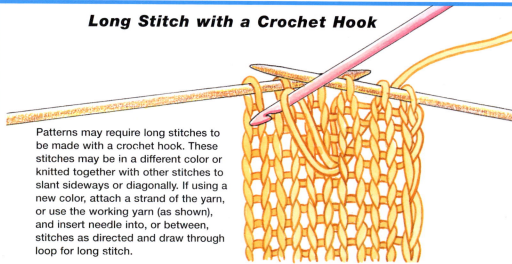

### Long Stitch with a Crochet Hook

Patterns may require long stitches to be made with a crochet hook. These stitches may be in a different color or knitted together with other stitches to slant sideways or diagonally. If using a new color, attach a strand of the yarn, or use the working yarn (as shown), and insert needle into, or between, stitches as directed and draw through loop for long stitch.

# long stitch and crossed stitch

**■ crossed stitch**

**1** **Stitch crossed to right on knit rows.** Work to spot for crossover, skip first stitch on left needle and reach pass it to knit second stitch on left needle, then knit skipped stitch, sliding both worked stitches off left needle.

**2** **Stitch crossed to left on knit rows.** Skip first stitch on left needle and reach behind it to knit back loop of next stitch, then knit into front of skipped stitch; slide both stitches off left needle.

**3** **Stitch crossed to right on purl row.** Skip first stitch, purl next stitch, then purl skipped stitch and slide both off left needle.

**4** **Stitch Crossed to left on purl row.** Skip first stitch and, reaching behind it, draw out loop of second stitch and purl it, then purl skipped stitch and slide both stitches off left needle.

# continental knitting

In some European countries, people knit with their hands and yarn held in a different position from the one more commonly used in the United States.

Some people may find it more comfortable to use this technique because you can keep the work close to your body, maintaining a more erect position. Try it to see which method works best for you. Either method should give good results, if followed correctly.

## ■ how to cast on the stitches

**1** Form the first stitch with a running knot placed on needle so that ball of yarn is on right-hand side of needle.

**2** Wrap yarn from ball around middle finger of left hand, then over index finger. Pass yarn from yarn end around thumb as shown, holding thumb and index finger about 2 inches (5 cm) apart.

**3** Rotate thumb and yarn upward so free yarn end forms a ring around your thumb. Hold end securely with other fingers.

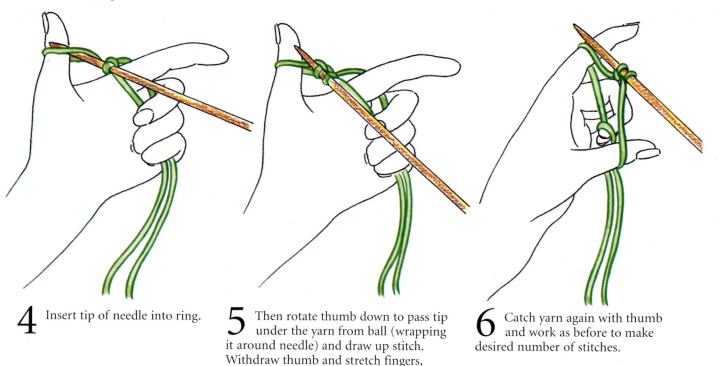

**4** Insert tip of needle into ring.

**5** Then rotate thumb down to pass tip under the yarn from ball (wrapping it around needle) and draw up stitch. Withdraw thumb and stretch fingers, pulling yarn gently to tighten knot.

**6** Catch yarn again with thumb and work as before to make desired number of stitches.

# continental knitting

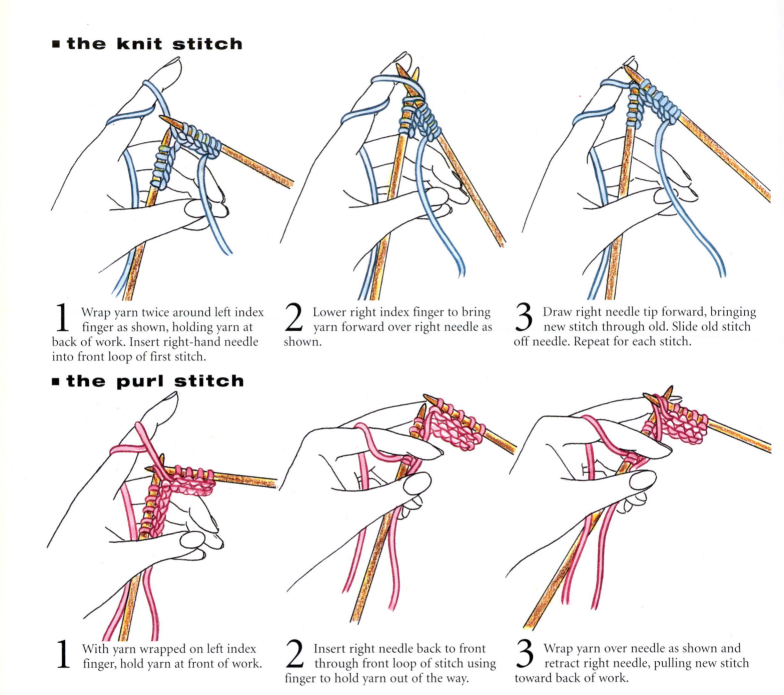

## ■ the knit stitch

**1** Wrap yarn twice around left index finger as shown, holding yarn at back of work. Insert right-hand needle into front loop of first stitch.

**2** Lower right index finger to bring yarn forward over right needle as shown.

**3** Draw right needle tip forward, bringing new stitch through old. Slide old stitch off needle. Repeat for each stitch.

## ■ the purl stitch

**1** With yarn wrapped on left index finger, hold yarn at front of work.

**2** Insert right needle back to front through front loop of stitch using finger to hold yarn out of the way.

**3** Wrap yarn over needle as shown and retract right needle, pulling new stitch toward back of work.

---

### *TIP*

Avid knitters often end up with leftover yarns—not enough for a sweater but too much to waste. One idea for using up cotton yarns is to make potholders or place mats in one color or several. In order to make them more colorful and cheerful, you can trim the edges with a border of cotton bias tape.

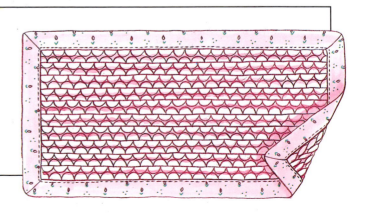

# ribbing started with tubular stitch 1

This stitch, also called double knitting, is worked on two needles and produces a double-sided work, making it reversible. It has two layers that can separate or form the start of ribbed edges.

■ **casting on yarn of a different color**

**1** With a contrasting color yarn, cast on half the number of stitches that you need, plus 1. Continue with yarn chosen for your work, as follows:

**2** **1st row:** Knit first stitch, *make a yarn over (see page 12, to bring yarn to front of work and wrap it over right needle to back, making a new stitch). Knit next stitch.

**3** Repeat from * across row. You should now have desired number of stitches. Turn work to work next row.

**4** **2nd row:** Work as follows: With yarn in front of work, slip first stitch as if to purl onto left needle without knitting it. Slip all stitches knitted on 1st row this way, alternating this step with the following one.

# ribbing started with tubular stitch 1

**5** With yarn behind work again, knit each yarn-over stitch added on 1st row.

**6** **3rd and 4th rows:** Work across, knitting each stitch slipped on previous row and slipping as if to purl each stitch worked on previous row.

**5th row:** Now work as usual in k1, p1 ribbing; continue in ribbing until piece is desired length.

**At the end of knitting,** remove colored yarn.

### Starting Edge for K2, P2 Ribbing

Cast on with contrasting color yarn and work first three rows as for tubular stitch 1. Then establish k2, p2 ribbing by working across all the stitches as follows: Skip first stitch, * knit (k) next k stitch and leave it on needle, skip 1 and k next stitch, leaving them on needle, bring yarn forward and purl first skipped stitch, dropping it and first k stitch from left needle, now purl 2nd skipped stitch and drop it and 2nd k stitch from left needle (k2, p2 worked), skip next stitch; repeat from * across row.

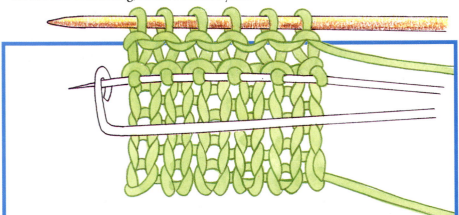

### Knitting the Edges

If you are using tubular stitch as the front edge on a cardigan and wish to continue knitting in stockinette stitch, use twice as many stitches. When the tubular stitch is removed from needles, it separates into two layers: the front knit side and the back purl side, as it faces you (see illustration).

You can get the opposite result (purl front and knit interior) if you work 2nd and 3rd rows as follows: **2nd row:** Purl stitches that will face outward; slip alternating stitches (that will face inward) without knitting them, holding yarn in front of work.

**3rd row:** Purl slipped stitches from previous row and with yarn in front, slip stitches that were worked on the previous row without working them. Once the double-knitted cardigan edge is completed, decrease the extra stitches by working 2 stitches together as one, and continue working in single layer as usual.

Using tubular knitting in this way to start ribbing gives the ribbing an attractive and stable beginning edge. It gives kl, p1 and k2, p2 ribbing the desired elasticity as well as the stability.

Tubular knitting is also useful when you want to start a stockinette stitch piece without forming an edge. The tubular stitch will prevent the edge from rolling up.

There are two ways to cast on the stitches for the tubular stitch: with a contrasting color yarn, as shown, or with the same yarn you will knit. Both work well.

The first time you try tubular stitch, you may find it difficult, especially the first few rows. Practice until you are familiar with the technique. Do not get discouraged, for once you learn it, this stitch is very easy, and it is a technique worth knowing.

# tubular stitch 2

**■ casting on with the same yarn used for knitting**

**1** Hold needle in your right hand. With the same yarn you want to use for knitting, form a loop on needle. Hold in left hand the yarn that comes from ball (yarn A); hold the other yarn end (B) with right hand.

**2** With left hand, wrap yarn A around needle forward and over needle, bringing it down behind needle.

**3** With right hand, bring yarn B under needle from behind to front so that it wraps around yarn A, forming second stitch (front stitch).

**4** With left hand, wrap yarn A again around needle (as in step 2).

**5** With right hand, bring yarn B in front of new loop and around under needle to back, forming third stitch (back stitch). Repeat steps 2 through 5 to make desired number of stitches. Make an even number of stitches; one will be dropped in step 9.

**NOTE:** Left hand always moves working yarn A to form new stitch, while right hand completes stitch by moving yarn end B alternately forward or backward.

# tubular stitch 2

**6** Stitches cast on in this way appear as alternating front stitches and back stitches.

**7** Holding needle in left hand, begin by slipping back stitch as if to purl, without working it, and knit next front stitch.

**8** Continue by slipping next back stitch as if to purl, knit next stitch.

**9** Continue working in this manner, alternating stitches, across row to last stitch, but do not work this last stitch (started as a single loop); drop it off from left needle.

**10** Continue to work rows in this manner, alternating stitches to knit slipped stitches of previous row and slip worked ones. Once you have finished knitting, close work (see next section). Then gently pull at loop formed by dropped stitch on first row, undoing beginning yarn.

# closing the tubular stitch

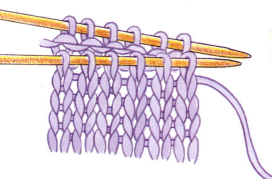

**T**he double or tubular stitch requires a particular stitch for closing the work, known as the weaving stitch or the kitchner stitch. You will need a blunt-tipped yarn needle to do it.

## ▪ knit closing

When the last row of tubular knitting is done, cut yarn, leaving an end long enough for weaving stitches together.

Slip stitches off knitting needle; stitches will automatically separate into a front and a back section; put a needle into each group of stitches.

**1** Notice that the front needle holds outer knit stitches and the other needle holds inner purl stitches (as they face you).

**2** Thread long yarn end in yarn needle. Insert yarn needle (as if to knit) into first stitch on front needle and slide stitch off needle.

**3** * Insert yarn needle into first 2 stitches on back needle, entering stitches as if to purl, then let both stitches slide off back needle.

**4** Bring yarn needle back to front needle, entering from front to back of first stitch (dropped from needle in step 2), then insert needle in next knit stitch as if to purl and slide both stitches from front needle.

**5** Return to back needle, enter from far back (exterior) into stitch that was just dropped from needle in step 4 and into next stitch from interior out back, letting it drop off needle. Repeat from * across, weaving all stitches together.

# closing the tubular stitch

## ■ purl closing

**1** Insert threaded yarn needle as if to knit into first stitch on front needle and slide it off needle.

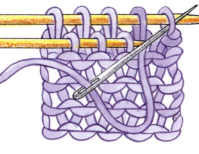

**2** * Return to back needle, entering first stitch on interior of work as if to knit and slide it off back needle.

**3** Insert yarn needle into next stitch from back to interior and let it slide off back needle.

**4** Bring yarn needle back to front needle, entering from interior into front stitch dropped in step 1, then enter next stitch on front needle from front to interior, sliding it off front needle. Continue repeating from *, weaving all stitches together.

---

### Closing with a Single Needle

Closing tubular knit can also be done leaving your work on only 1 needle. The method is similar and may be easier to follow for some knitters.

First, cut off yarn, leaving long end for working; yarn end emerges from second stitch (back stitch). Thread yarn end into yarn needle.

**1** Insert yarn needle from exterior (knit side of stitch) through first stitch, then second stitch from interior (purl side of stitch), and slide both stitches off knitting needle.

**2** Insert yarn needle from exterior into first front stitch just dropped and from interior on next stitch on knitting needle, and slide both stitches off knitting needle.

Continue in this manner, entering stitch just dropped from exterior and next stitch on needle from interior, and dropping both stitches, until all stitches are worked off.

# single and double increases

To increase means to add one or more stitches to your work. The increases can be divided between internal, within the current edges of the piece, and external, which are made at the edges of the work, either at the beginning or at the end of a row.

## ■ internal increases

**1** **Single increase.**
Knit same stitch twice, first through front loop as usual, then with stitch still on left needle; reach behind work to knit into back loop of same stitch (working 2 stitches in 1); slide old stitch from left needle. You can also increase purl stitches by purling into front and back of same stitch.

**2** **Increase toward the right.** With tip of right needle, lift stitch beneath stitch you wish to knit and knit it, then knit stitch on needle. You can also increase purl stitches working into stitch and one below it.

**3** **Increase toward the left.** Knit stitch on needle as usual without sliding it off needle, then, with tip of left needle, lift stitch beneath one just worked and knit it. You can also increase purl stitches this way.

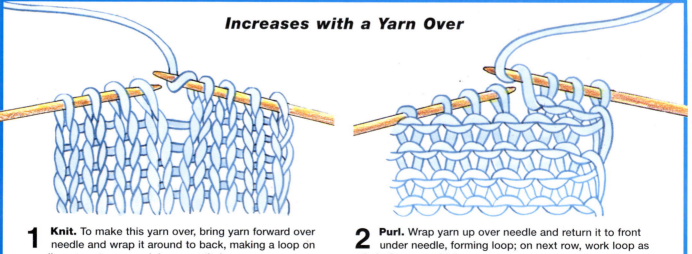

### Increases with a Yarn Over

**1** **Knit.** To make this yarn over, bring yarn forward over needle and wrap it around to back, making a loop on needle; on next row, work loop as stitch.

**2** **Purl.** Wrap yarn up over needle and return it to front under needle, forming loop; on next row, work loop as stitch. See page 12 for more ways to make a yarn over.

23

# single and double increases

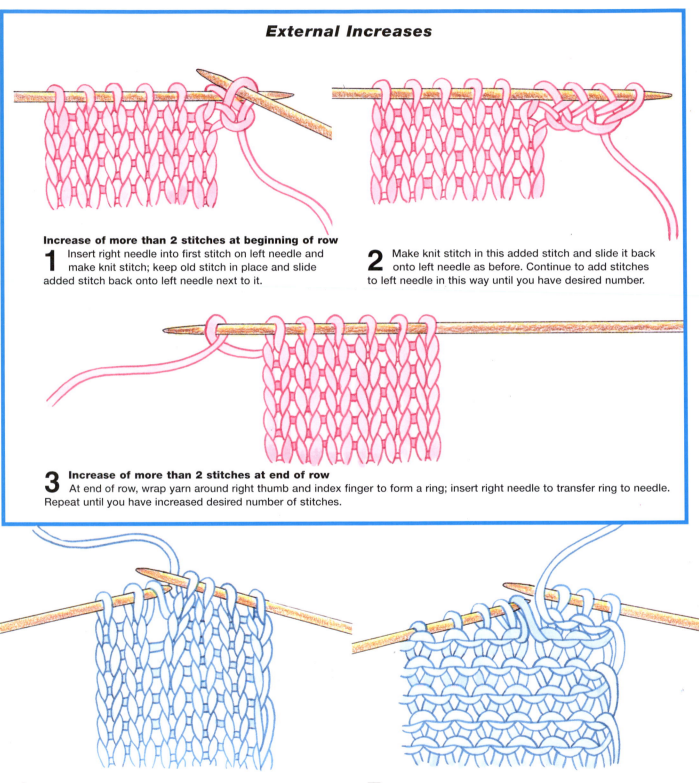

### External Increases

**Increase of more than 2 stitches at beginning of row**

**1** Insert right needle into first stitch on left needle and make knit stitch; keep old stitch in place and slide added stitch back onto left needle next to it.

**2** Make knit stitch in this added stitch and slide it back onto left needle as before. Continue to add stitches to left needle in this way until you have desired number.

**3** **Increase of more than 2 stitches at end of row** At end of row, wrap yarn around right thumb and index finger to form a ring; insert right needle to transfer ring to needle. Repeat until you have increased desired number of stitches.

**4** **Invisible increase on knit rows.** Use tip of left needle to pick up strand of yarn that connects stitch on right needle to next one on left needle.

Knit this stitch in twisted fashion, inserting needle into back loop to knit it.

**5** **Invisible increase on purl rows.** Use tip of left needle to pick up strand of yarn connecting stitch on right needle to next one on left needle, putting it on left needle.

Purl this stitch in twisted fashion, inserting needle into back loop to purl it.

# symmetrical increases

These increases are generally used to add a certain number of stitches on the inside of the work. These have various decorative effects and are normally made every other row on the front of your work.

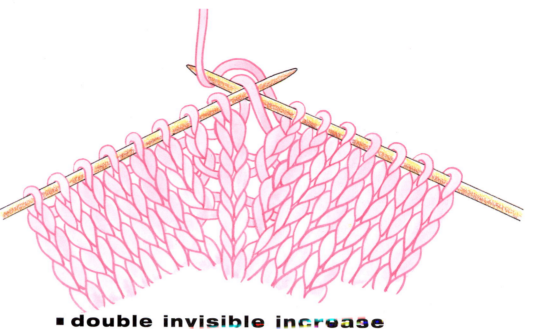

## ▪ double invisible increase

With tip of right needle, lift connecting stand of yarn just before center stitch and place resulting loop onto left needle; knit this new stitch in twisted manner (through back loop).

Knit center stitch; repeat with connecting yarn just after center stitch.

## ▪ repeated double increase

Knit stitch before center one and then make left increase in same stitch as follows: Insert left needle into stitch to pull up strand under this stitch, knit the loop as stitch.

Knit center stitch, then make right increase as follows: Insert right needle into next stitch to pull up strand under this stitch and knit it. Knit stitch on needle.

## ▪ double open-work increase

Knit to center stitch, make a yarn over (see page 12).

Knit center stitch, make another yarn over. On next row, work yarn-over loops as stitches.

# symmetrical increases

## ▪ inserted increase with holes

Knit to center stitch, then with right needle pull up connecting strand between stitch just worked and center; place this loop onto left needle and knit it as stitch.

Knit center stitch, then pull up next connecting strand as before and knit it.

---

### Increases Symmetrically Repeated

**1 Simple single**
Increase by knitting into front, then back of same stitch (see page 23). Symmetry is obtained by working the increase on the 3rd stitch from the beginning of the row and on 4th stitch from end of row. (**NOTE:** The first and last stitches on the row are shown as slip stitches in these illustrations and elsewhere in the book.)

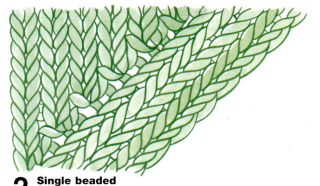

**2 Single beaded**
Knit a stitch, leaving it on left needle, and then bring yarn forward to purl back loop of same stitch; return yarn to back to continue knitting. Symmetry is obtained by working increase on 3rd stitch from beginning of row and on 3rd stitch from end.

**3 Single inserted**
With left needle, pull up connecting strand between last stitch on right needle and next one on left needle, and knit it. Symmetry is obtained by working increase after 3rd stitch at beginning of row and just before 3d stitch from end of row.

**4 Single open-work**
Increase by making a yarn over (see page 12). Symmetry is obtained by working increase after third stitch at beginning of the row and just before third stitch from end of row.

# single and double decreases

**D**ecreases, used for shaping the sweater, can be internal (within a row) or external (at the edges). They can be used to shape side seams, armholes, sleeves, and neck opening.

## ■ internal decreases

These can be done at any point during the work. However, decreasing within a row does not alter the selvage edge; it may require adjustments to keep continuity of a fancy pattern stitch.

**1 Decrease 2 knit stitches together (k2tog)**
Insert right needle into first 2 stitches on left needle and knit stitches together as one. This decrease will slant right.
If you knit 2 stitches together through back loops, they will be twisted, making a decorative decrease that slants left.

**2 Decrease 2 purl stitches together (p2tog)**
Insert right needle into first 2 stitches on the needle and purl stitches together as one. On following knit row, decrease will slant right.

**3 Knit stitch with slip stitch passed over (psso)**
Slip stitch as if to knit, without knitting it, to right needle, and knit next stitch on left needle. (Or slip stitch as if to purl, as shown, for a twisted stitch decrease, if you prefer.)
With tip of left needle, lift slipped stitch, pass it over knitted stitch, and let it drop from needle. Decrease will slant left.

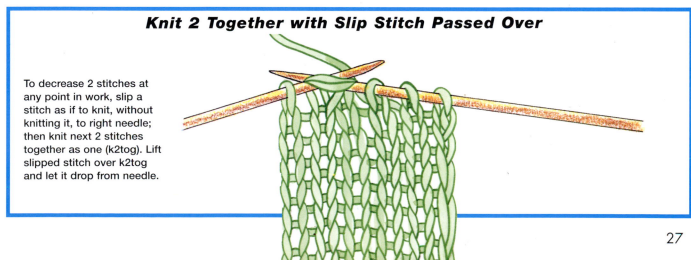

### Knit 2 Together with Slip Stitch Passed Over

To decrease 2 stitches at any point in work, slip a stitch as if to knit, without knitting it, to right needle; then knit next 2 stitches together as one (k2tog). Lift slipped stitch over k2tog and let it drop from needle.

# single and double decreases

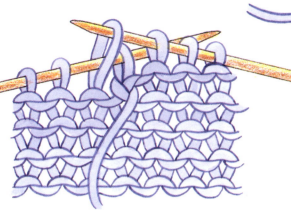

**4** **Purl stitch with unworked stitch passed**
For decrease, purl stitch as usual, then slide new stitch back onto left needle.

With tip of right needle, lift second (unworked) stitch on left needle up and over first (worked) stitch and let it drop off needle. Slide first stitch back to right needle.

**5** **Double slip stitch passed over yarn over**
Slip 2 stitches onto right needle without knitting them, then make yarn over.

Lift 2 slipped stitches up and over yarn over.

## Binding Off (External Decreases of Multiple Stitches)

### On Knit Row
Knit first 2 stitches. With tip of left needle, lift first stitch worked over second and drop it (first decrease made), knit next stitch, and repeat process until all desired decreases are made. If you are binding off all stitches, work to end of row; cut off yarn and draw yarn end through last stitch to tighten.

### On Purl Row
Work as for knit row, but purl stitches.

### With Unfinished Stitches
To avoid unattractive jogs when stitches are bound off in successive steps, work across row to where stitches are to be bound off. *Turn work without binding off. Keeping the unworked stitches on needle, slip first stitch on left needle (shown as twisted stitch on diagram), work to end of row. Turn and work back to where next set of stitches was to be bound off; repeat from * until all stitches to be bound off are excluded.

Bind off all the stitches left on left needle. Or you can knit across them all and place them on a holder to weave them to the adjoining edge (as for a shoulder).

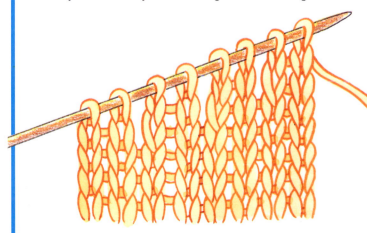

# symmetrical decreases 1

These decrease stitches are widely used for shaping raglan sleeves or corners or on a border when you make decreases on both sides of a central stitch.

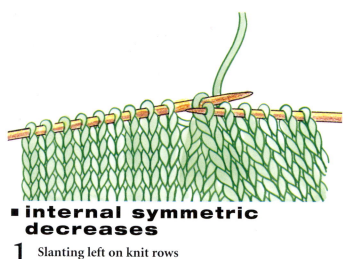

### ■ internal symmetric decreases

**1** **Slanting left on knit rows**
On each decrease row, always work same number of stitches at edge (before or after 2-stitch decrease is made) to give uniform and symmetric edge. Work decrease on 2 stitches as follows: slip 1 stitch, knit 1 stitch, pass slip stitch over knit 1 and drop it.

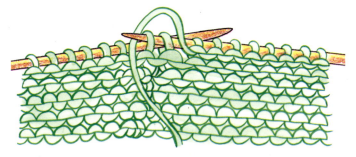

**2** **Slanting left on purl rows**
Keeping uniform edges, decrease by purling 2 stitches together as one.

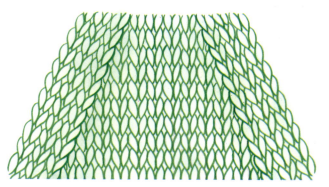

**3** **Slanting right on knit rows**
Keeping uniform edges, decrease by knitting 2 stitches together as one.

**4** **Slanting right on purl rows**
Keeping uniform edges, decrease on 2 stitches as follows: purl first stitch and return it to left needle; with tip of right needle, lift next stitch (unworked) on left needle and pass it over worked stitch and drop it from right needle. Slip worked stitch back to right needle.

**5** The illustration shows symmetrical decreases, slanting left at the beginning edge and right at ending edge. They can be worked on either the right or wrong side of work. They should be in opposite directions on same row and all rows on one project should be consistent to look symmetrical.

# symmetrical decreases 1

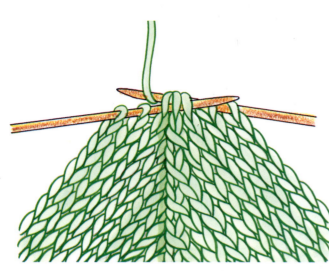

## ▪ double decreases with central rib stitch

**1** **Slanting left on knit rows**
Work decrease in center of piece on 3 stitches by knitting 3 stitches together through back of stitches; decrease will form a twisted stitch.

**2** **Slanting right on knit rows**
Insert right needle, starting with third stitch on left needle, then second and first stitches, to knit them together as 1 stitch.

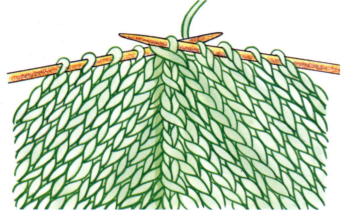

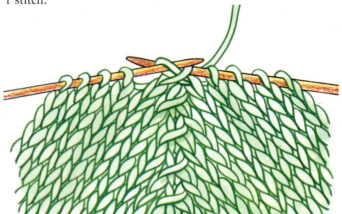

**3** **Pass slip stitch over decrease on knit rows**
Decrease on 3 stitches by slipping 1 stitch to right needle without working it, knit next 2 stitches together as one (k2tog); then with left needle lift slipped stitch up and over k2tog, letting it drop off needle.

**4** **Double slip stitch slanting right**
Decrease on 3 stitches as follows: Slip first stitch to right needle without working it, knit next stitch, then pass slipped stitch over one just worked and drop it from right needle. Return worked stitch to left needle and pass next stitch (unworked) on left needle over worked one and drop it. Slide remaining stitch back to right needle.

### Double Slip Stitch with Vertical Center

Decrease on 3 stitches as follows: Insert right needle through both center stitch and first stitch as if to knit them together and slip them both onto right needle without knitting them. Knit next stitch on left needle, then pass slipped stitches over knitted one; remaining stitch becomes a new center stitch. This decrease is good for a V neck.

# symmetrical decreases 2

## ■ decorative symmetrical decreases

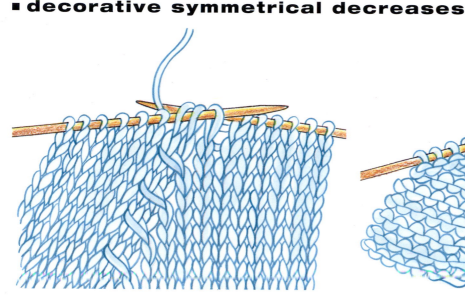

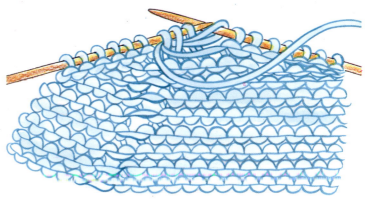

**1** **Crossed with right slanting edge on knit rows**
Keeping a uniform number of stitches (usually 2 or 3) at edge, decrease on 3 stitches as follows: skip first stitch and, with right needle, reach behind work to knit second and third stitches together as one (stitches are twisted), then knit first (skipped) stitch as usual. Slide worked stitches off left needle. One stitch has been decreased.

**2** **Crossed with left slanting edge (worked on purl rows)**
Keeping uniform edge, decrease on 3 stitches as follows: Skip first stitch and, with right needle, purl second and third stitches together as one without sliding them off left needle; purl first (skipped) stitch. Slide worked stitches off left needle. On knit side of work, edge slants left.

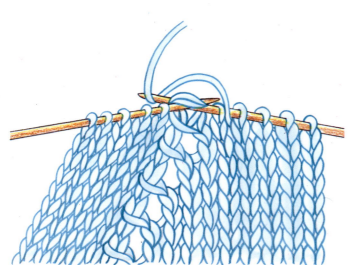

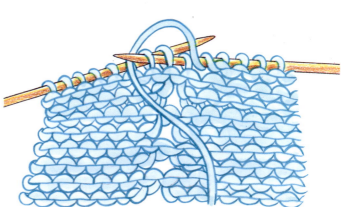

**3** **Lacy knit with right slanting edge on knit rows**
Keeping edge uniform, decrease on 3 stitches as follows: Bring yarn forward, slip next stitch without working it, wrap yarn over needle to back (forming yarn over: yo), insert right needle as if to knit into second, then first stitch on left needle and knit the 2 stitches together as one (k2tog); pass slip stitch over k2tog and let it drop from needle. Work yo as a stitch on next row.

**4** **Lacy knit with left slanting edge (worked on purl rows)**
Keeping edge uniform, work decrease on 3 stitches as follows: Wrap yarn back over needle and return to front to form yarn over (yo), slip next stitch without working it, purl next 2 stitches together as one (p2tog); pass slip stitch over p2tog and let it drop from needle. Work yo over as a stitch on next row.

# symmetrical decreases 2

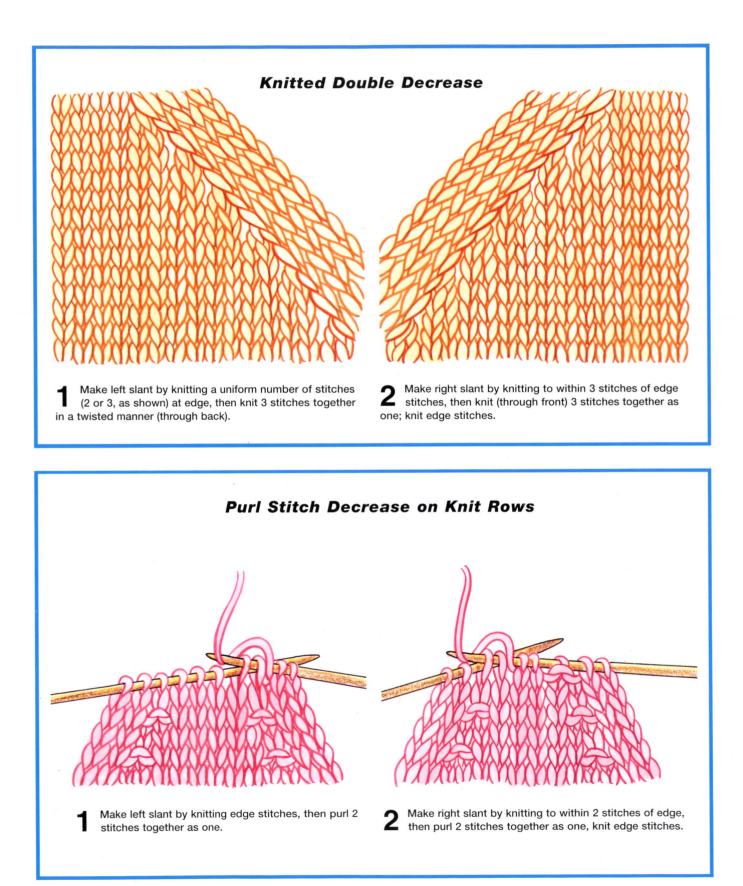

## Knitted Double Decrease

**1** Make left slant by knitting a uniform number of stitches (2 or 3, as shown) at edge, then knit 3 stitches together in a twisted manner (through back).

**2** Make right slant by knitting to within 3 stitches of edge stitches, then knit (through front) 3 stitches together as one; knit edge stitches.

## Purl Stitch Decrease on Knit Rows

**1** Make left slant by knitting edge stitches, then purl 2 stitches together as one.

**2** Make right slant by knitting to within 2 stitches of edge, then purl 2 stitches together as one, knit edge stitches.

# binding off

**K**nitting is generally finished by binding off the stitches following the pattern of the piece (knit stitches are knitted and purl stitches are purled) and working just loosely enough to keep the elasticity of the work.

### ■ binding off (knit stitch)

Knit 2 stitches, then, with tip of left needle, lift first stitch and pass it over second stitch; drop it from needle. Knit next stitch and repeat procedure; repeat across row to last stitch. To fasten off, see next page

### ■ binding off (purl stitch)

Purl 2 stitches, then, with left needle, pass first stitch over second and drop it. Purl next stitch and repeat procedure; repeat across row to last stitch. To fasten off, see next page.

### ■ slanted binding off

Use for smoothly-shaped edge when you bind a few stitches on several rows for shaping (as for neck or shoulder shaping).

Bind off on every other row: Bind off first set of stitches; on return row, leave last stitch (unworked) on left needle (see illustration). Turn work. On next (bind off) row, unworked stitch is now on right needle, work next stitch and pass unworked stitch over it for first bound-off stitch. Complete binding off.

Binding off for right edge is worked on knit (or right side) rows; binding off for left edge is worked on purl (or wrong side) rows.

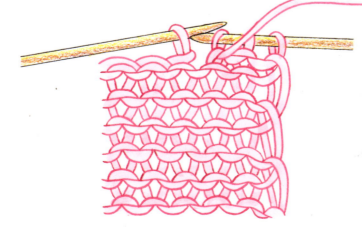

# binding off

## ■ slanted turned binding off

Use as for slanted binding off.

On every other row work to stitches you want to bind off, bring yarn to front of work, slip one stitch, take yarn to back and return slipped stitch to left needle without knitting it.

Turn work and work back across now shortened row.

Repeat procedure until all stitches are done, then bind them all off at same time.

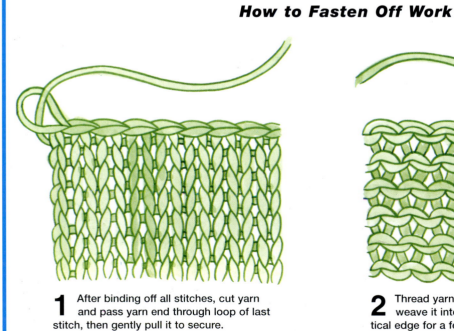

## ■ twisted binding off

Knit first 2 stitches together as one in twisted manner (through back loops).

* Slip resulting stitch back on left needle and knit it together with following stitch. Repeat from * across row.

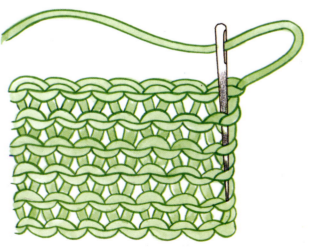

---

### How to Fasten Off Work

**1** After binding off all stitches, cut yarn and pass yarn end through loop of last stitch, then gently pull it to secure.

**2** Thread yarn end in yarn needle and weave it into back of stitches along vertical edge for a few inches.

# v neck

Like other neck openings, this one can be finished by knitting up or by sewing the edges. Both need to be done with great care so they lie flat without stretching.

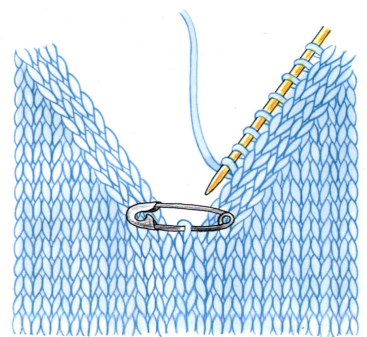

## ■ v neck with k1, p1 ribbing

**1** On first row of V-neck shaping, place center stitch on a safety pin to hold until needed. Work each side of neck separately with a separate ball of yarn. Decrease 1 stitch on each side every 2 or 4 rows, just before or after the edge stitches at each neck edge. When all decreases are completed, work even (keeping same number of stitches) until you finish shoulders. Pick up stitches along each neck edge (see page 51) and place them on needles so needles meet tip to tip. (A double-pointed (dp) needle may facilitate this.)

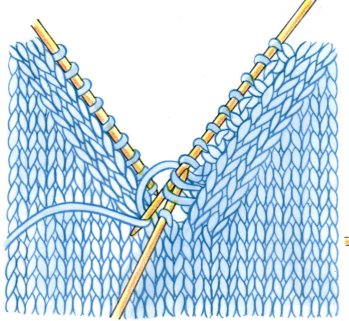

**2** Work border in k1, p1 ribbing as follows: On right side rows, knit together the 2 stitches that precede the center stitch. Transfer center stitch from holder to a dp needle.

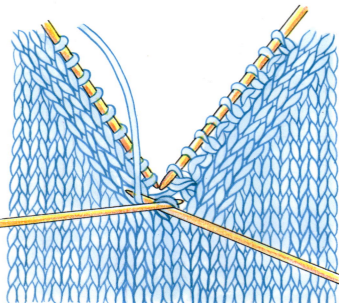

**3** Knit center stitch; on next needle, knit together 2 stitches following center stitch; work in ribbing as established to end. On wrong side rows, work as established, purling together 2 stitches (decrease made) before center stitch. Purl center stitch, then next stitch. Slip this last stitch back to left needle, slip next stitch on left needle over it (another decrease); slip decrease stitch back to right needle and continue ribbing as established.

## ▪ v neck with k2, p2 ribbing

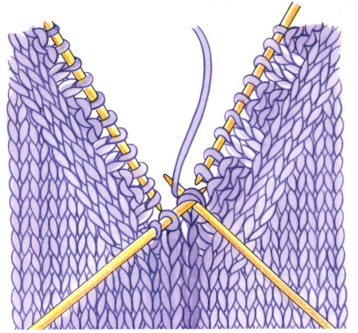

**1** Place 2 center stitches on a holder. To work neckband, pick up stitches and work k2, p2 ribbing as follows: Transfer center stitches to a dp needle. On right side rows, knit stitch before first center stitch and first center stitch together as one.

### Overlaid Ribbing

For assembled garment, pick up stitches around entire neck edge with circular needle, starting and ending at V. If only front is being worked, work each neck edge separately from V to shoulder. Work back and forth in k1, p1 ribbing (no decreases) for the desired width. Bind off all stitches in ribbing. At V, overlap ends and neatly stitch in place with yarn and yarn needle.

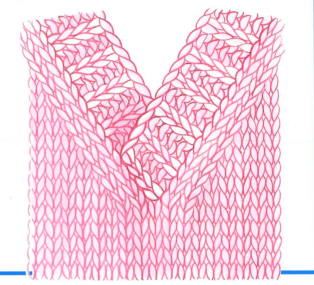

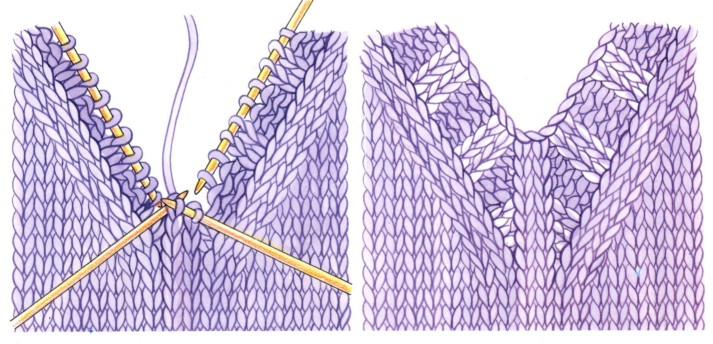

**2** Skip next center stitch without knitting it. Work next stitch and pass skipped stitch over it, letting it drop. Work in ribbing as established to end of row. On wrong side rows, work to 4 center stitches (including ones just before and after original two), purl first 2 stitches together in a twisted fashion; purl together next 2 stitches, then rib to end.

# polo neck

This is the classic neck opening used for sports garments.

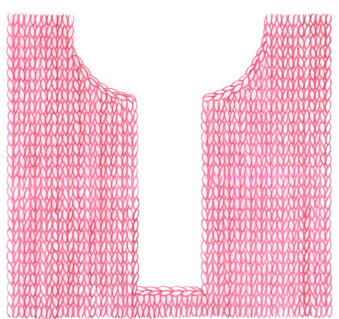

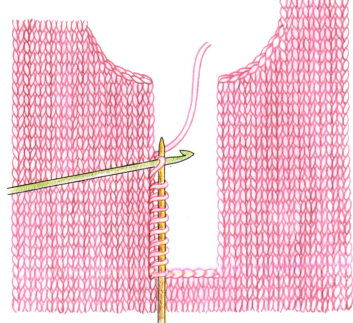

**1** At center front, bind off desired number of stitches (opening should be about 1 inch/2½ cm wide). Attaching separate yarn for each side, work evenly (without decreasing) on each side to neck shaping. Shape neck and complete shoulders.

**2** With a crochet hook, pick up stitches on one side of opening and transfer them to needle.

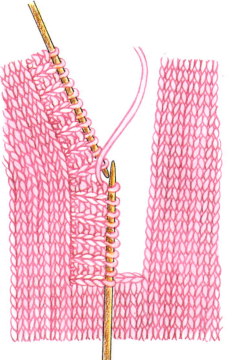

**3** Work stitches in k1, p1 ribbing until border width is about half the width of panel opening. Make 3 evenly-spaced buttonholes on next row as follows: Yarn over (yo) needle, work next 2 stitches together as one. On next row, work yo as a stitch, continuing to rib as established until border is same width as opening. Bind off.

**4** Work other opening edge to correspond, omitting buttonholes. Bind off. With yarn and yarn needle, neatly sew buttonhole border to bottom edge of opening with backstitch.

# polo neck

**5** On wrong side, neatly sew bottom of solid (button) border on top of first one.

**6** To add collar, use crochet hook to pick up stitches around neck edge and transfer to double-pointed needles (or circular one), leaving stitches of 2 borders free.

**7** Work collar in k1, p1 ribbing for width desired. Bind off loosely, or knit last 4 rows in tubular stitch, as shown, closing stitches with yarn needle.

# square neck

The square neck is a true classic of knitted garments. The neck edge is filled in with a knitted-on decorative border. The sailor collar version has a border made as the collar is knitted.

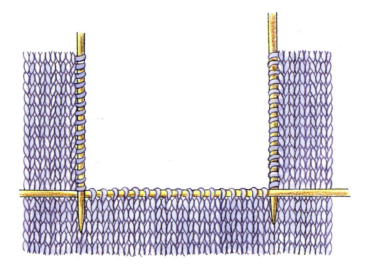

**1** Place stitches for neck opening (including those needed for side borders) onto holder to be worked later. Work remaining stitches on each side with separate yarn to complete shoulders. Use crochet hook to pick up stitches for border and transfer them to double-pointed (dp) needles, using a dp needle for each edge.

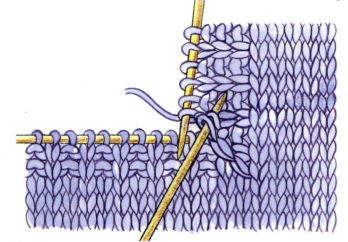

**2** Work stitches in k1, p1 ribbing, designating a center knit stitch for each corner. Work 3 stitches at each corner (corner stitch and ones just before and after) as follows: Insert needle into first 2 stitches as if to knit them together and slip them without working them onto another dp needle.

**3** Knit next stitch and pass 2 slipped stitches over it (corner stitch remains). Repeat at each corner.

**4** Repeat these decreases every other row for border width. Bind off or knit last 2 rows in a tubular stitch, as shown, closing stitches with a yarn needle.

## The Sailor Collar

A square neck is suitable for a sailor collar. Starting with the desired (uneven) number of stitches for the collar, work in moss stitch (k1, *p1, k1; repeat across on each row), or other simple pattern for about ½ inch (1 cm). Keeping first and last ½ inch (3 or 5 stitches) in pattern stitch, work remaining center stitches in stockinette stitch (knit 1 row, purl 1 row) until piece measures 3 to 4 inches (8 to 10 cm) from beginning row. Now start pattern stitch edge for neck opening, including side borders and keeping all borders the same width.

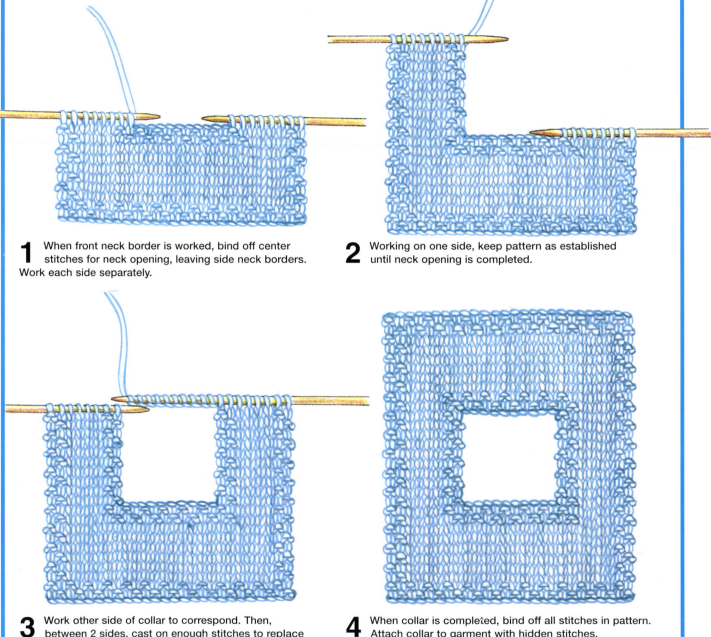

**1** When front neck border is worked, bind off center stitches for neck opening, leaving side neck borders. Work each side separately.

**2** Working on one side, keep pattern as established until neck opening is completed.

**3** Work other side of collar to correspond. Then, between 2 sides, cast on enough stitches to replace those bound off. Work back of collar to correspond to front.

**4** When collar is completed, bind off all stitches in pattern. Attach collar to garment with hidden stitches.

# round neck

This is the neck opening most widely used in knitting. It can be finished by knitting a neckband or by attaching a collar made to fit the neck opening of the completed garment.

■ **round neck**

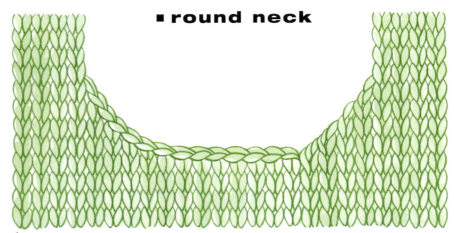

**1** Determine the desired size and number of stitches to be reduced for neck opening (multiply inches/cm by gauge). To start opening on front, bind off half the number of stitches to be reduced at center of row. Working one side at time, decrease remaining stitches (half on each side) by binding off 1 or 2 stitches every other row until you have completed decreases. Complete shoulder.

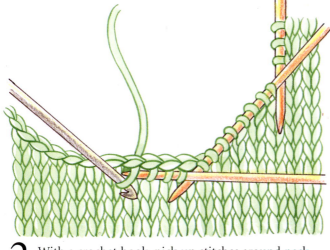

**2** With a crochet hook, pick up stitches around neck opening by keeping yarn at back of work and inserting hook into center of each stitch; draw up a loop and transfer it to needle (double-pointed or circular needles are easiest for working neckband).

**3** You can also pick up stitches directly with needles by holding yarn at back to wrap each stitch; divide stitches equally onto 4 dp needles.

**4** Work in k1, p1 ribbing for desired number of rows. Bind off in ribbing or work last few rows in tubular stitch as shown; close stitches with yarn needle.

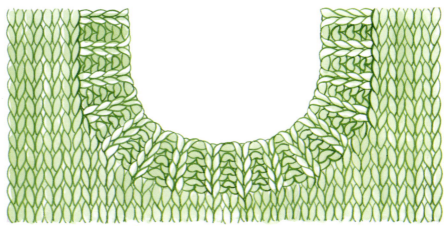

## Round Neck with Applied Border

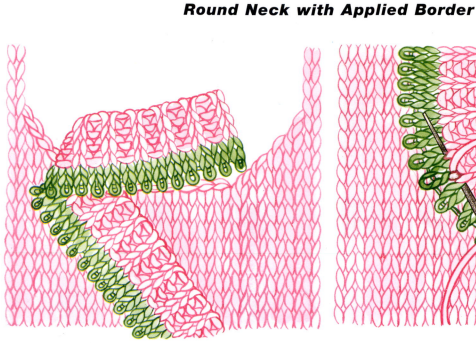

**1** **Simple border in k1, p1 ribbing**
Work shaping for round neck as described on previous page. Then determine number of stitches needed for border to fit neck opening. Make border by starting it with tubular stitch, then working stitches in k1, p1 ribbing for desired width. Finish with several added rows of stockinette stitch worked in contrasting color yarn.

**2** Pin border in place around neck opening with colored edge just overlapping garment. With matching yarn and yarn needle, neatly sew border to neck edge, sewing stitch by stitch (with backstitch) around last matching row of stitches. Be sure loop of each stitch is attached to neck edge.

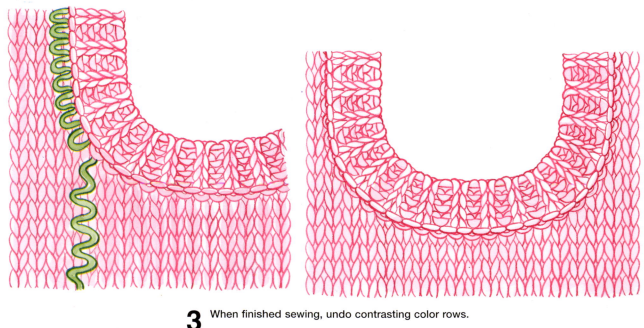

**3** When finished sewing, undo contrasting color rows.

# neck openings, shoulders, and sleeves 1

**P**roperly done neck openings and shoulders help determine the elegance and success of a knitted garment. The style of their shape depends on the yarn you are using and the function of the garment you want to knit.

## ■ rounded sleeves

Rounded sleeves are traditional and widely used; they can be adapted to many types of garments. Sometimes the armhole is bigger on front, but usually the front and back are equal. To calculate stitches you need to decrease for armholes, subtract stitches for shoulders and neck opening from total number of stitches on front or back, then divide number of remaining stitches by 2: these will be stitches to decrease for each armhole. Start by binding off 3 or 4 stitches at once, then 2 stitches, and finally decrease 1 stitch every other row until you decrease the desired number of stitches. For sleeve shaping, make the same decreases indicated for front and back (if front and back differ, match one edge to front, one to back; reverse for other sleeve). Then continue to round top of sleeve by decreasing 1 stitch every other row on each edge. Make these decreases symmetrically until curve of top is adapted to that of armhole and has reached desired length. Bind off all remaining stitches.

Armholes of the front and back will be same if the front and back of the sweater are the same. If the front of the sweater is larger than the back, half of the stitches to be reduced should be bound off at beginning of each armhole.

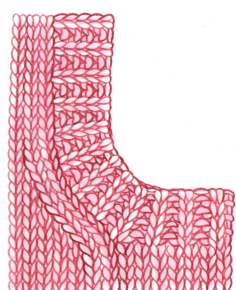

### *Round Armhole for a Vest or Sleeveless Sweater*

When you are knitting a sleeveless sweater with a finished edge, the armhole needs to be bigger to accommodate the armhole band.

# neck openings, shoulders, and sleeves 1

## ■ raglan sleeves

Raglan sleeves are often used for sports garments and rather heavy garments. To calculate the number of stitches to decrease on front or back (which usually are equal), divide number of stitches into 3 parts: 1 slightly smaller part for neck opening and 2 equal parts for shoulders. The number of stitches for each "shoulder" is the number of decreases needed for each armhole. Start by binding off 3 or 4 stitches once at each edge, then continue decreasing 1 stitch on each side every other row, leaving desired number of edge stitches before and after each decrease. You will be eliminating all stitches (but edge stitches) as you complete neck and raglan shaping. Work raglan sleeves to correspond. Start shaping with enough stitches on needle to be able to decrease the same number of stitches at raglan sleeve edges as were decreased for raglan armholes of back and front, plus a few stitches for neck opening edge (enough for about 1½ inches/4 cm). When raglan shaping is completed, bind off remaining stitches.

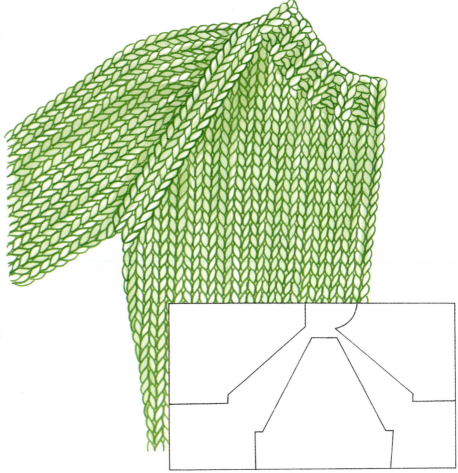

## Classic Shoulders

For a custom fit and finish, shape back shoulders and leave front shoulder edge straight.

Instead of binding off back shoulder stitches in steps as usual and connecting shoulders with a seam, work as follows: Omit any front shoulder shaping and place all front shoulder stitches on a holder. On back shoulder, work shaping rows as usual, but instead of binding off the stitches, transfer them to double pointed (dp) needle, using separate needle for each step. Transfer front stitches from holder to a needle and, using weaving stitch (see pages 21–22), join edges together in an invisible seam.

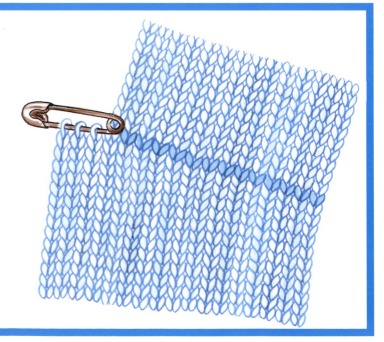

## ■ saddle sleeves

Work front and back armholes like regular armholes until 1–1½ inches (2½–4 cm) shorter than normal length to shoulder; top of shoulder is covered by upper part of saddle sleeve.

Top of sleeve is shaped in usual rounded manner until only enough stitches (measuring 2 to 3 inches/5 to 7½ cm across) remain to fill out omitted shoulder sections of front and back. Mark last row worked with safety pin. Continue working these stitches until piece measures (from marker) the same as shoulder edge of front or back to neck opening. Bind off stitches. This bound-off edge will be part of neck opening. This type of sleeve nicely shapes shoulders and can have a decorative look if worked in contrasting colors or with a vertical stripe.

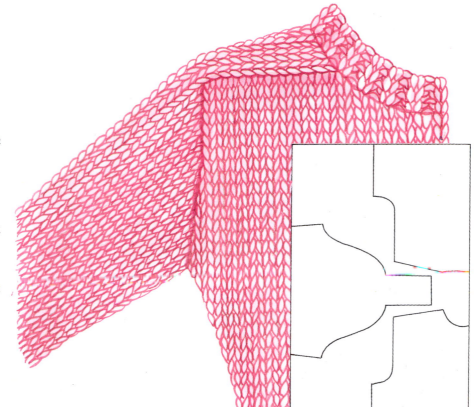

## ■ raglan without sewing

This type of raglan is good for baby clothes, because there are fewer lumpy seams.

Knit front (or 2 fronts), back, and 2 sleeves separately until you reach armholes. Arrange pieces as shown and distribute all stitches onto double-pointed needles, placing markers on needle to indicate start of each section.

Knit around if front is a single unit, or knit back and forth in rows if front is divided in two (a circular needle can also be used in this case). Make decreases regularly on each section, within edge stitches for section. (Always work edge stitches in stockinette st regardless of pattern stitch used for rest of garment.)

At end, bind off neck stitches and sew side and underarm seams.

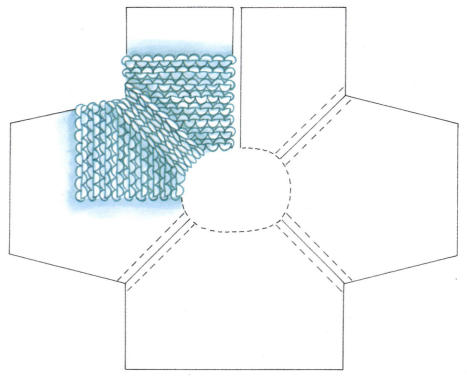

# neck openings, shoulders, and sleeves 2

## ■ semi-raglan sleeves

Armholes on front and back are worked as classic raglan on lower half as follows: Bind off desired number of stitches once on each side, then decrease 1 stitch on each side every 2 (or 4) rows, leaving desired number of edge stitches before and after decreases; work until armhole is half desired length to shoulder. Now work even (without decreases) to shoulders. Shape shoulders, binding off in several steps. On sleeves, work armhole decreases same as for front and back, then bind off all remaining stitches. Semi-raglan sleeve is good for sports garments; it unites the practicality of raglan sleeve to the shape of rounded sleeve.

### Open Shoulders

On both front and back, work neck shaping as usual, then work shoulders as follows: Leaving 2 edge stitches beyond decrease, decrease at neck edge every row until all stitches (but edge stitches) are decreased; bind off edge stitches. Work neckband as desired, then, at armhole edge, overlap shoulder flaps as shown to finish.

### Buttoned Shoulders

Work back shoulder shaping using slanted binding off (see page 28) as follows: Start shaping about ½ inch (1 cm) below normal and work off an even a third of the shoulder stitches every other row 3 times.

Finish neck and shoulder edges with k2, p2 ribbing on back and front. Work small buttonholes on front shoulder ribbing. Sew buttons on back to correspond.

# wristbands 1

Wristbands are the typical edge for the long sleeves of a sweater. They can be made as you knit the sleeve or by picking up the stitches after the sleeve is done. Double knitting them makes them sturdy.

## ■ wristband made by picking up stitches

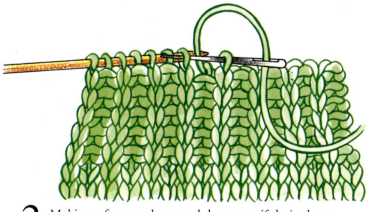

**1** Cast on sleeve stitches with contrasting color yarn. When sleeve is completed, use yarn needle to undo stitches of beginning row, passing them onto knitting needle as you undo them.

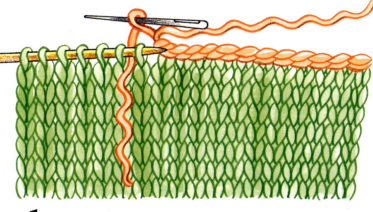

**2** Making a few evenly-spaced decreases, if desired, on first row, work wristband in ribbing or double knitting. When wristband is the desired length, bind off stitches as usual in pattern, or for tubular knits, use yarn needle as if to purl on both layers to close edge.

## ■ wristband in k1, p1 ribbing

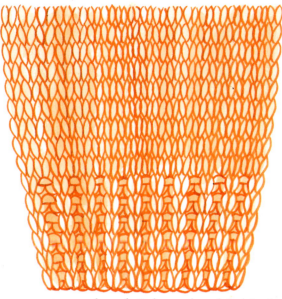

Cast on an uneven number of stitches and work in k1, p1 ribbing for length desired (generally 2–4 inches/5–10 cm; fuller sleeve needs longer length). When ribbing work is completed, continue working sleeve. To seam wristband edges, sew as if to purl, picking up a stitch for each side.

## ■ wristband in k2, p2 ribbing

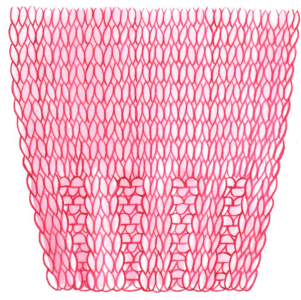

Cast on a number of stitches in multiples of 4 + 2.

Work in k2, p2 ribbing, beginning and ending each right side row with 2 knit stitches, for desired length, then continue on sleeve.

To finish, sew wristband edges, using yarn needle as if to purl, picking up a stitch from each side for an invisible seam.

# wristbands 1

## ■ wristband with full sleeve

Cast on desired number (uneven number) of stitches to work in a k1, p1 ribbing; work to desired length.

To work sleeve, knit evenly-spaced increases on first row as follows: * knit 3 stitches, insert tip of right needle under strand of yarn connecting last worked stitch to the next one and transfer it to left needle. Knit this loop as a stitch in the twisted manner. * Repeat from * to across row. On next row, purl all stitches. For a less full sleeve, work more stitches between increases.

## ■ wristband with a cord

Good for baby clothes, this is worked by casting on the number of stitches for the desired width of the sleeve; no additional increases will be needed.

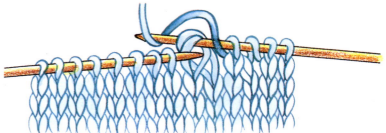

**1** Knit 3 rows (garter stitch), then continue for about ½ inch (1½ cm) in stockinette stitch, ending with purl row. Next row: Work eyelets as follows: Knit first stitch, * work yarn over (yo), knit 2 stitches together *; repeat from * across row, ending with knit stitch. Purl next row, working yo loops as stitches.

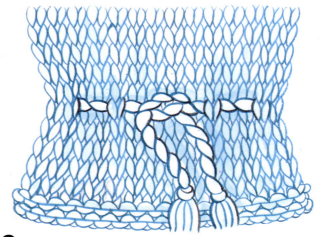

**2** When garment is completed, weave a yarn cord or ribbon through eyelets at wrists for tie.

### How To Make a Twisted Cord

Cut 3 or 4 strands of yarn, each cut to a length three times as long as you want the finished cord to be.

Holding strands together, fold them in half and tie 2 ends together to form a long loop; hook knotted end over door knob or hook.

Stretch this loop to its limit and, at looped end, insert a pencil; twist yarns, making them rotate in same direction.

When strands are well twisted, fold them in the middle (with both ends together); the yarns will rotate automatically to form the cord. Bind ends with a small knot.

## ■ wristband with a straight border

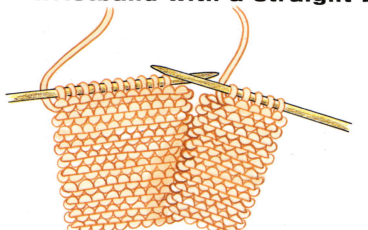

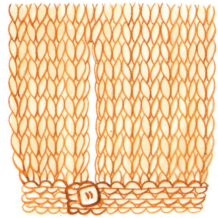

**Prepare opening**: Cast on a third of the stitches needed for first sleeve row, cast on 2 more stitches for opening edge; with separate ball of yarn, cast on 2 stitches, then remaining two-thirds of stitches. Work each part separately for about 2 inches (5 cm). On next row, join sections, binding off the 2 added stitches at each opening edge and working across remaining stitches with same yarn. Complete sleeve, sew sleeve seam, then turn under opening edges and sew in place on wrong side. Work other sleeve to correspond, reversing position of parts.

**Make wristband**: Along bottom edge of sleeve, pick up stitches for wristband, casting on a few extra stitches at one end for overlap. Knit a few rows (garter stitch) and work a buttonhole on a middle row on the overlap (yarn over, k2 stitches together). Complete band and bind off all stitches. Sew on button.

## ■ wristband with shaped border

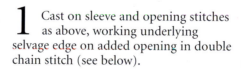

**1** Cast on sleeve and opening stitches as above, working underlying selvage edge on added opening in double chain stitch (see below).

**2** To work border, pick up stitches along wrist edge and front opening edge. Knit each row (garter stitch), working 2 small buttonholes along opening edge and shaping at corner as follows: On each right side row, knit to corner, increase 1 stitch, knit corner stitch, increase 1 stitch, knit to end; on wrong side rows, purl corner stitch and knit all other stitches. When band is completed, bind off all stitches.

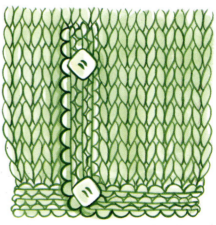

**3** Place front edge (with border) overlapping back opening edge. With yarn and yarn needle, neatly sew edges together on wrong side. Sew on buttons.

**Selvage in double chain stitch**: On knit rows, slip edge stitch without knitting it, purl the stitch next to it. On purl rows, purl both stitches.

# wristbands 2

## ■ sewn on wristband

**1** Cast on enough stitches for twice the desired band width (band will be folded in half); work in stockinette stitch (knit 1 row, purl 1 row).

When band almost fits wrist edge of sleeve, shape end as follows: Decrease 1 stitch at beginning and end of each row; at the same time, make 2 buttonholes on 1 row, each buttonhole the same distance in outer edges. Gently ease edges so the sleeve fits unshaped length of wristband with point extended.

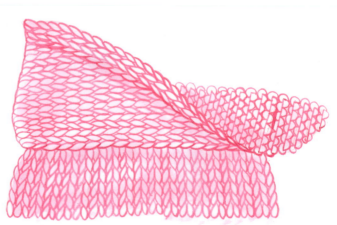

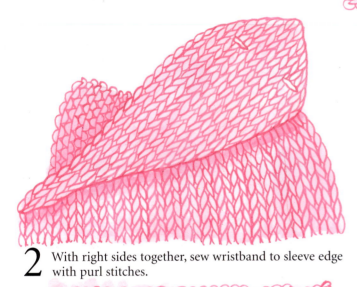

**2** With right sides together, sew wristband to sleeve edge with purl stitches.

**3** Fold wristband in half, right sides together, and sew shaped tip edges with purl stitches.

**4** Turn wristband right side out, fold it half lengthwise, and sew band edge in place along sleeve joining on wrong side. Sew short straight ends of the wristband together with invisible stitches.

Sew buttonhole edges together with buttonhole stitch; sew button to opposite end of band to correspond.

### Connecting with Invisible Sewing

Work on right side of work, attaching edges of stockinette stitch pieces, or pieces in pattern stitch with stockinette stitch edge stitches.

Attach yarn and thread it in yarn needle. Always sewing between edge stitch and next stitch, work stitch on one side of seam, then on other side being joined. Alternate from side to side, carefully drawing yarn through to make edges meet perfectly.

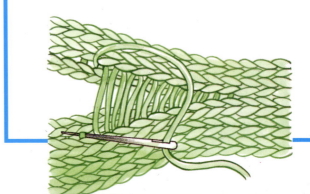

The collar completes and refines the neck opening of a garment. It can have a variety of shapes depending on the fashion style of the moment and the chosen pattern.

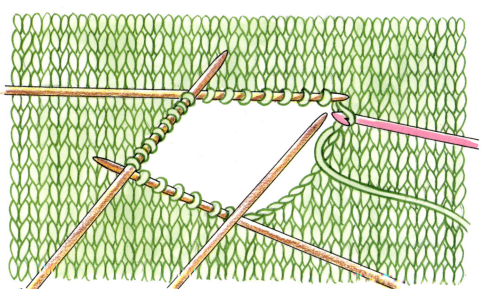

## ■ turtleneck

Good for outdoor garments, such as ski sweaters, it is worked on a rather large round neck opening.

**1** With a crochet hook, pick desired number of stitches around neck opening, transferring them to a double pointed (dp) needle as you go; divide stitches evenly on 4 dp needles.

**2** With the fifth dp needle, knit around in k1, p1 ribbing for desired length.

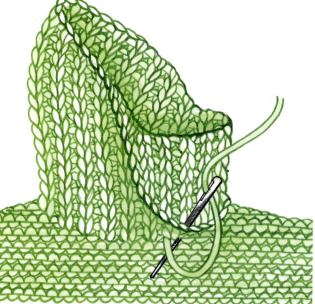

**3** Bind off stitches in ribbing, then fold turtleneck in half to wrong side of work. Turn garment inside out and sew turtleneck edge to neck edge.

### Turtleneck

A turtleneck can also be folded toward the right side of a garment after binding off stitches loosely, or knitting the last few rows with needles one size larger.

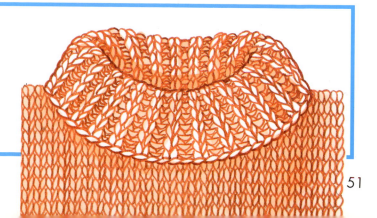

51

# collars 1

## ■ collar with simple lapels

This collar is good for jackets. To have it come out well, make an actual-sized paper pattern, clearly and precisely marking pattern for beginning of V neck and shaping of neck edges.

**1** Work to start of V neck for left front, ending at front edge. Begin collar as follows: Work 3 stitches in moss stitch (k1, p1, k1; on following rows, k the p stitches as they face you, and p the k stitches). At front edge, continue to work 1 more stitch in moss stitch on each row until pattern section is about 4¼ inches (11 cm) wide.

**2** Continue, without adding more pattern stitches, until 6 inches (15 cm) above start of V neck. At the front edge, bind off half the pattern stitches and complete row as established.

**3** At end of next row (front edge), cast on same number of stitches as just bound off on last row. Working new stitches in moss stitch, work even until pattern section is about 11 inches (27 cm). Bind off for shoulders, keeping lapel stitches on the needle.

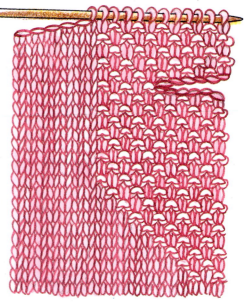

**4** Work short rows to shape remaining stitches for the back collar as follows: Continuing in pattern, work across half the stitches, turn work and work back across same stitches. *Work in pattern across all stitches for 4 rows. Repeat short rows as before. Repeat from * until back collar measures 3½ inches (9 cm) along inner edge. Place stitches on a holder.

**5** Work right front to correspond, reversing shaping. Complete and assemble garment. Join the back collar stitches at center back with weaving stitch and attach inner collar edge to back neck opening.

# collars 2

## ■ joined collar and lapel

**1** The lapel is made as you work the front. At the front edge, cast on the same number of extra stitches for the interfacing as you cast on the bottom of the jacket front; mark front edge by working first interface stitch with a purl stitch or a moss stitch, as shown.

Work front to start of armhole. Shape armhole and, at the same time, shape, increasing 1 stitch at outer edge at regular intervals, depending on size desired (a few stitches wider than lapel).

**2** Work in this manner to start of neck shaping. Place lapel stitches and interfacing on a holder, then shape neck opening. Complete shoulder.

**3** Place stitches from holder onto needle and bind off all stitches of lapel and interfacing to last few stitches (4 shown).

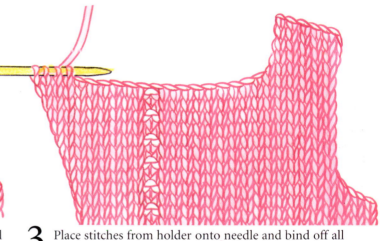

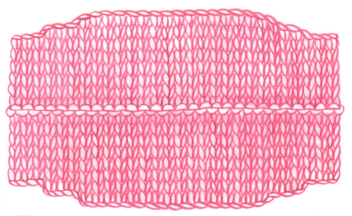

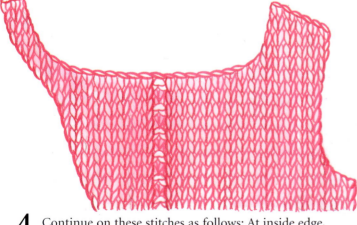

**4** Continue on these stitches as follows: At inside edge, decrease to correspond to neck shaping worked for front; at the same time, at outer edge, increase 1 stitch for each stitch decreased for neck shaping, maintaining a uniform number of stitches. (When folded back, interfacing should match neck shaping.) Work even to shoulder, then bind off all stitches.

**5** To work collar, measure back neck edge and cast on appropriate number of stitches. At each end of next 2 or 3 rows, increase number of stitches to equal decreases of the front neck. Work even until piece measures two-thirds of the interfacing width, then, on next wrong side, knit row across to form a fold line. Continue to work as before to correspond to lower half of collar, decreasing same number of stitches on last few rows as were added to first rows. Bind off stitches.

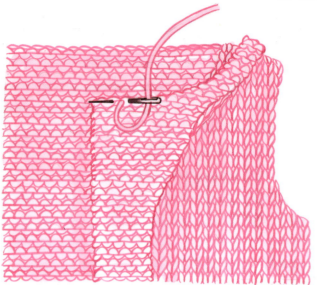

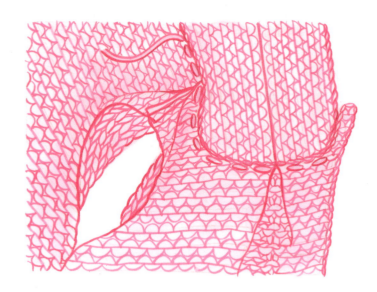

**6** Sew shoulder seams. Fold interfacing along front fold line. Match neck edges and sew very front edge near fold line.

**7** Open interfacing so wrong side is toward you. With collar opened flat, position it so that the fold line lines up with fold line of interfacing on each front. Sew collar edge to neck edge, from one end to opposite end with backstitch.

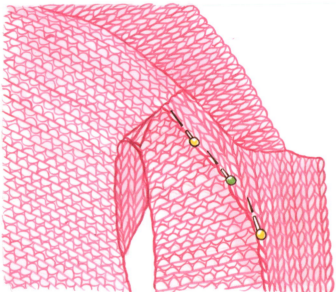

**8** Fold collar along fold line toward wrong side of garment; sew free edge of collar to neck edge. Sew end of interfacing to shoulder seam on each side.

### TIPS

- To avoid having loose side edges in a garment knitted in garter stitch (knit every row), always purl first stitch of each row; this will form a sturdy edge that will make joining pieces together easier.

- When you have almost finished a ball of wool, always attach new yarn at beginning of row to avoid knots in your work. Save yarn ends for sewing finishing touches.

**9** Turn jacket right side out as shown. This tailored collar is good for suit jackets. To do it well requires careful planning and execution. Making an actual-sized paper patterns before beginning helps to assure that pieces will be the proper size and will fit together.

# hems 1

**A** knitted hem is a layer of knitting folded and attached to the wrong side of a garment. There are a number of techniques that can be used to make hems for a variety of garments.

Generally, the edge that forms the hem is marked off with a fold line made with slip stitches, or a purl row worked on the right side of work, or a row of eyelets (cat tooth hem).

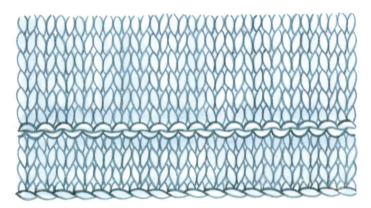

## ▪ purled folding line

Using smaller needles, cast on the desired number of stitches. Work hem in stockinette stitch to desired depth. On right side row, purl (instead of knit) across. Change to the larger needles you plan to use for rest of garment to continue working.

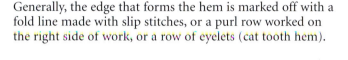
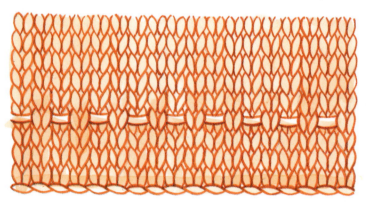

## ▪ fold line with slip stitches

Use this technique when you want a less distinct fold line for the hem. With smaller needles, work hem in stockinette stitch to desired depth. On next knit row, work as follows: Knit 1 stitch, *then with yarn in front of work slip 1 stitch as if to purl, return yarn to back and knit 1 stitch. Repeat from * across row, ending with a knit stitch. Change needles.

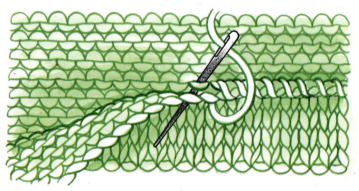

## ▪ how to sew hem in slip stitch

To finish garment, fold hem to wrong side. With yarn threaded in yarn needle, work across from right to left, making each stitch through back of a stitch on garment body and in corresponding stitch of hem. Sew just loosely enough that sewing line is not visible on front.

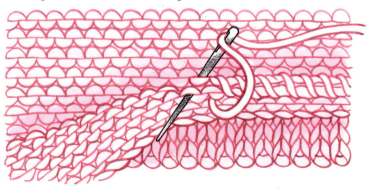

## ▪ how to sew hem in hidden stitch

Fold hem to wrong side. As you sew, fold top of hem toward you and make stitches through back of garment and back of hem, slightly left of the previous stitch and just below hem edge. Release folded top of hem to cover sewing line.

## Cat Tooth Hem

**1** With smaller needles, cast on stitches with contrasting color yarn. Change to main color. Work hem in stockinette stitch to desired depth. On next right-side row, work eyelet row as follows: * Knit 2 stitches together as one (k2tog), yarn over (yo); repeat from * across row, ending with knit stitch. Change to larger needles you plan to use for garment. Work yo loops as stitches on next row.

**2** When work is completed, use yarn needle to undo colored stitches of beginning row and transfer them to knitting needle as you undo them.

**4** Then stitch through 2 corresponding stitches on back of garment. Repeat steps 3 and 4 working stitches 2 by 2 and alternating between hem and garment.

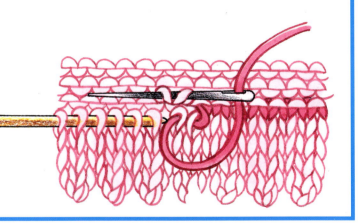

**3** Fold hem to wrong side along eyelet row and sew it in place with weaving stitch as follows: Insert yarn needle back through first stitch on needle and bring it out front through next stitch on needle.

## ■ curved hem

**1** Cast on stitches with contrasting color yarn. Change to main color and work in stockinette stitch to twice desired depth for hem, using smaller needles for middle rows. Use yarn needle to undo colored stitches and transfer them to knitting needle.

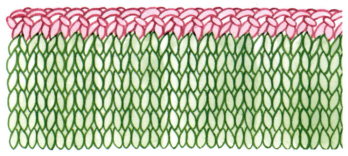

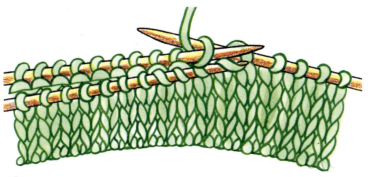

**2** Fold hem in half, wrong sides together. Hold 2 needles close together and knit row as follows: Insert needle into first stitch on each needle and knit 2 stitches together as one; repeat across row. An invisible curved hem will result. Use smaller needles for the rows near fold or the bottom will fan out.

# hems 2

**■ hem with picked up stitches**

**1** With contrasting color yarn, cast on half the stitches needed. Change to main color and work in stockinette stitch for 7 or more rows.

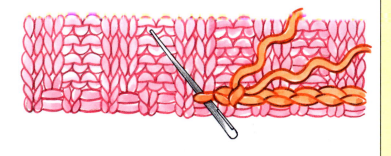

**3** With yarn needle, undo colored stitches. This hem is elastic and is good for ribbed patterns.

**2** On next row, with purl side toward you, work with desired pattern stitch (k2, p2 ribbing is shown) as follows: Work 2 stitches from left needle, then 2 stitches from first row of hem, alternating this way across row to make hem. Continue in pattern.

**■ vertical hem with slip stitches**

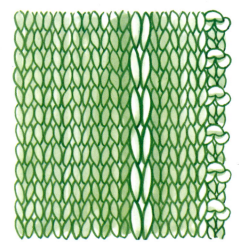

**1** Cast on stitches for garment and hem. Work in stockinette stitch, but work selvage stitch hem in moss stitch and form fold line by slipping stitch (at inner edge of hem) without knitting it on each knit row. Purl rows normally.

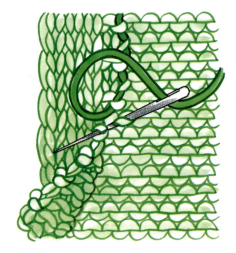

**2** When garment is completed, fold hem under and sew it to wrong side, stitching through back loops on garment and selvage edge of hem. Work just loosely enough to prevent hemline from showing.

## Edge in a Lacy Cable Pattern

This edge is good for women's and children's sweaters that have no shaping along the front.

Cast on the desired number of stitches that is a multiple of 3. Work across in lacy cable pattern as follows:

**1st (wrong side) row:** * Purl 1 stitch, work yarn over (yo), purl 1 stitch, knit 1 stitch; repeat from * across row (increases made on row).

**2nd row:** * Working yo loop as a stitch, purl 1, knit 3; repeat from * across.

**3rd row:** * Purl 3, knit 1; repeat from *across.

**4th row:** * Purl 1, slip 1 as if to purl without knitting it, leaving yarn in front of work knit 2 together as one (k2tog), pass slipped stitch over k2tog; repeat from * across. (You should now have on needle the same number of stitches that you cast on.) Repeat these 4 rows for pattern stitch to desired depth for border. (As shown, pattern is worked twice.)

Keeping border same width as lower border, separate (with marker) the vertical border stitches, using enough stitches for 2 (as shown) or more pattern repeats. Continue to work vertical border in pattern and remaining stitches in stockinette stitch. Complete your work.

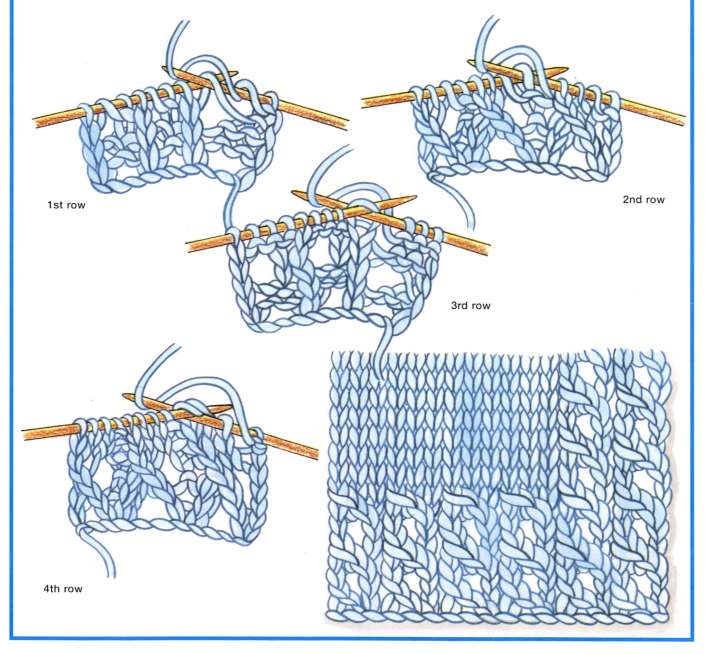

1st row

2nd row

3rd row

4th row

# edgings 2

## ■ the picked up edges

Picked up edges are used along curved edges, or when you want to knit edging in the opposite direction from the one in which the garment is worked. Use a crochet hook and/or knitting needle to pick up stitches along the edge being finished.

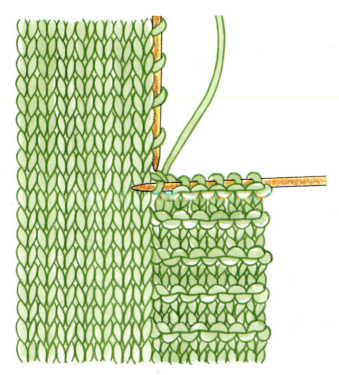

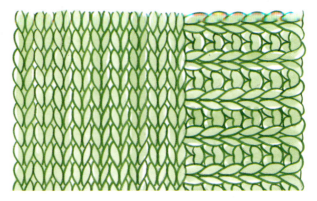

**1** **Edging in Moss Stitch**
Pick up needed stitches along edge and work them in moss stitch for the desired width. Bind off all stitches in pattern as usual, or with a crochet hook (see below).

**2** **Edging in Garter Stitch, Picked Up Vertically**
To make edging worked in same direction as garment was worked, cast on stitches for edging, and, on another needle, pick up edge stitches (1 stitch for every 2 rows) along garment edge.

Knit edging in garter stitch and as you work, on every other row, knit together last stitch of edging and corresponding picked-up stitch of selvage.

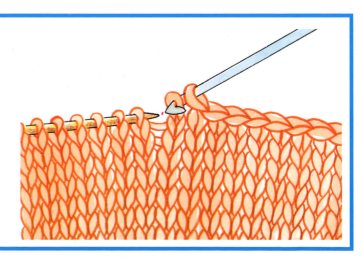

**3** **Edging in K1, P1 Ribbing**
Pick up stitches for edging and work in k1, p1 ribbing for the desired width, working last 4 rows in a tubular stitch. Finish by closing stitches.

---

### Binding Off with Crochet Hook

To bind off, use crochet hook a little bit thicker than the yarn. Pick up first stitch with crochet hook, then draw second stitch through first (first stitch bound off).

Continue to draw each stitch, one at a time, through loop remaining on hook until all stitches are bound off. Cut yarn and draw yarn end through last loop to secure. With yarn needle, weave end into work.

## Lacy Edging

Pick up uneven number of stitches. Work edging, for desired depth, in lacy pattern as follows:

**First 3 rows:** Purl across.
**4th row (right side):** Knit 1 stitch, *work yarn over (yo), slip 1 stitch as if to knit (without knitting it), knit 1 stitch, pass slip stitch over knitted one; repeat from * across.
**Next 3 rows:** Purl across.
Bind off all stitches with crochet hook (see previous page).

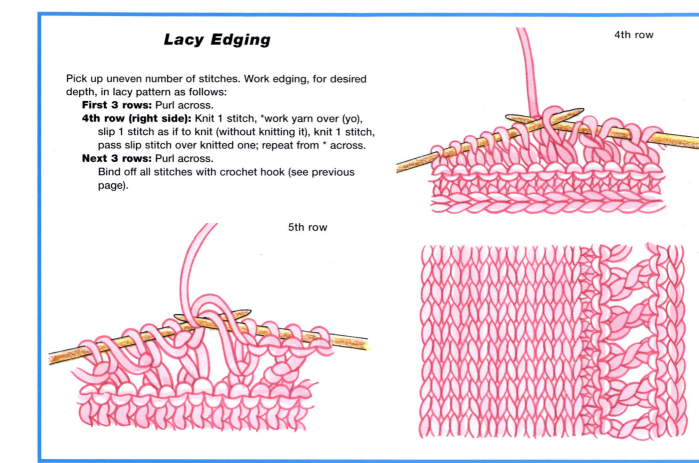

4th row

5th row

## Edging in Ladder Stitch

**1st row:** * Knit 2 stitches, purl 2 stitches; repeat from * across to end of row.

**2nd row:** Continue to work in k2, p2, but shift pattern by 1 stitch to left (for example, if 1st row ended with purl 2, the 2nd row will start with purl 1 stitch, then knit 2, purl 2, and so on). Continue to work in k2, p2, shifting stitches on each row and always slanting pattern in same direction for desired depth.

To finish edging, bind off all stitches with crochet hook (see previous page).

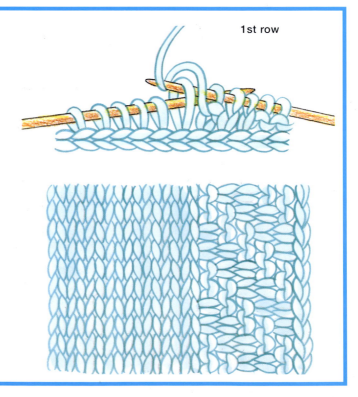

1st row

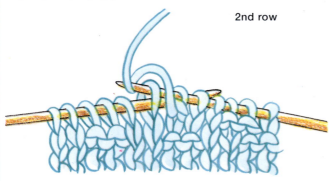

2nd row

# selvages and picking up stitches

The selvages are the side edges of the knitted work. They can be done in different ways based on their intended use: for sewing seams, for finishing, or for picking up stitches.

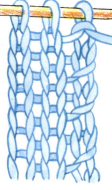

## ■ garter stitch selvage

Use for seam edges on stockinette stitch pieces.

On knit rows, work first and last stitch in twisted purl.

On purl rows, work first stitch in a very tight purl and slip last stitch without knitting it.

## ■ beaded selvage

Use with seams sewn with backstitch, regardless of knitted pattern stitch. On every row, slip first stitch as if to knit without knitting it and knit last stitch on row.

## ■ moss stitch selvage

Use for a firm and attractive edge.

On every row, work first and last 3 stitches as follows: Purl 1, knit 1, purl 1.

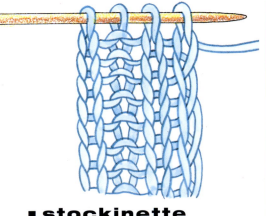

## ■ stockinette selvage

Use as an all-purpose selvage.

On right side rows, start with knit 2, purl 1; end row with purl 1, knit 2. (You can work first and last stitch on row in chain stitch, as shown at right, if you prefer.)

On wrong side rows, work stitches as they face you.

## Selvage Suitable for Picking Up Stitches

The chain stitch selvage works well for edges where you will pick up stitches for finishing. Chain stitch selvage can be worked in 2 different ways that give the same result.

**First (Italian) Method:** On right side rows, slip first stitch as if to knit without knitting it and knit last stitch.

On wrong side rows: Slip first stitch as if to purl without purling it and purl last stitch.

**Second (English) Method:** On right side rows, slip both first and last stitches without knitting them.

On wrong side rows: (Yarn is between first two stitches.) Purl all stitches across row, including first one.

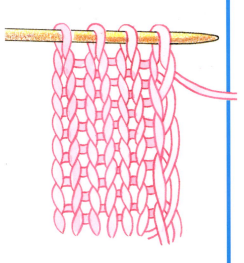

# selvages and picking up stitches

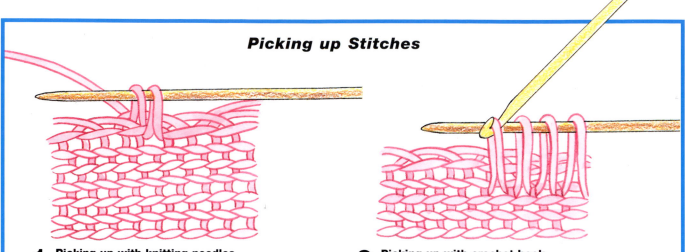

**Picking up Stitches**

## 1 Picking up with knitting needles

Each stitch of chain-stitch selvage corresponds to 2 rows, not 1, of knitting; remember to pick up enough stitches along edge to compensate for this, or picked-up edge will be too tight.

Pick up 2 stitches in 1 chain as follows: Insert needle under front loop of chain and knit it, repeat for back loop of same chain.

## 2 Picking up with crochet hook

Tuck knitting needle under your right arm when using crochet hook. Insert crochet hook through center of first stitch below selvage chain. Catch yarn on hook and draw up first stitch and transfer it to knitting needle.

If selvage is irregular, pick up stitches in second (not first) line of stitches at edge.

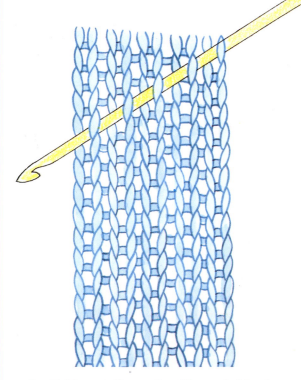

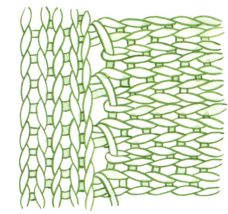

## PRACTICAL TIPS

If instructions don't indicate the number of stitches you need to pick up, make your calculation, based on the sample gauge.

Measure edge where stitches will be picked up, multiply number of inches by number of stitches per inch on sample gauge; the result is the number of stitches to pick up.

To work along side edge of piece, you generally need to pick up 1 stitch for every row or every other row if you are working an edging with the same pattern stitch as on the piece itself. Pick up 1 stitch every row if you are working edging with smaller needles than on piece.

To work in same direction as original piece (as for wristband), you generally need to pick up 1 stitch in every stitch, if you don't need to make decreases or increases.

## 3 Picking up diagonally with crochet hook

To pick up stitches on a slant (as for diagonal pocket), draw up stitches with crochet hook (as described above), working into stitch 1 row below previous one.

Diagram shows stitches that hook should go into.

# circular knitting

**K**nitting in the round can be done with a double-pointed needle set of four, or preferably five, needles, or with a circular needle. By knitting around, you eliminate seams.

## ▪ knitting with double-pointed (dp) needles

This is a good way to make a seamless neckband. Whether you cast on stitches to start, or pick up stitches around neck opening, working the rest of the neckband is the same.

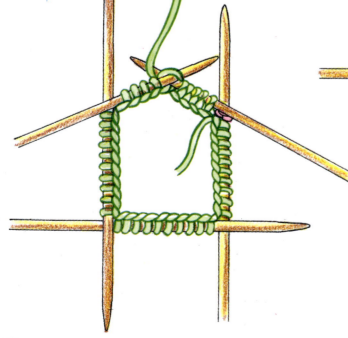

**1** Cast on or pick up a quarter of the stitches on 1 of 5 needles, then place another needle on top of first one (so it can be moved easily), and place another quarter of the stitches on this second needle, working with same yarn. Continue in this fashion until you have all the stitches you need, evenly distributed and untwisted, on 4 needles.

**2** Arrange 4 needles in a square, put a marker (colored loop of yarn) on needle after last cast-on stitch. Start knitting the first stitches, using fifth needle. Knit all stitches off first needle; use now emptied needle for knitting stitches of next needle, and so on until you have knitted all the started stitches back to marker.

**3** Be sure to mark beginning of the round (circular row), with a yarn loop or a safety pin in last stitch, moving it up each round. Proceed as described in step 2, knitting each new needle with needle just emptied, working around and around.

# circular knitting

## ■ knitting with a circular needle

**1** Using a same-sized straight needle, cast on desired number of stitches and transfer (slip) them without twisting onto circular needle. (You can also cast onto circular needle directly.) Use proper length of circular needle so stitches fit easily from tip to tip.

**2** Working back and forth as if using 2 needles, knit 1 row, turn work, and purl 1 row. As you go, slide piece to keep working stitches at needle tips.

**3** Do not turn after last row just worked. Place a marker on needle for start of rounds (circular rows) and knit around needle to starting marker. Do not turn work, but slip marker off needle.

**4** On next round, knit first stitch and place marker back on needle, then knit around. Continue to knit around and around and at start of each round, slip marker in place from left to right needle tip.

# correcting mistakes

When you knit, you may make mistakes. Follow the easy methods illustrated here and many of them will not be hard to fix.

## ▪ a dropped knit stitch

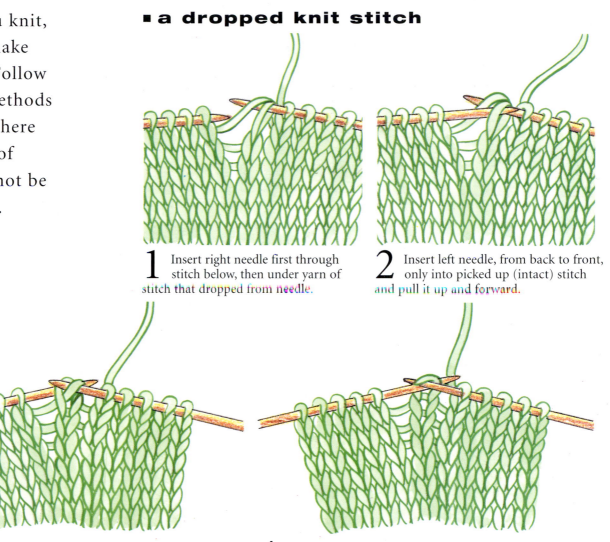

**1** Insert right needle first through stitch below, then under yarn of stitch that dropped from needle.

**2** Insert left needle, from back to front, only into picked up (intact) stitch and pull it up and forward.

**3** Slip this lifted stitch over yarn on right needle and let it fall from right needle, then from left needle. The stitch remaining is the dropped stitch restored, but facing wrong way.

**4** Insert left needle front to back into restored stitch, slipping it from right to left needle. Knit it as usual.

## ▪ error in garter stitch pattern

If an error happens while knitting garter stitch, undo corresponding stitch(es) directly above the error until you reach row with the error; undo error. Then with crochet hook catch stitch from front and work as described above if stitch needs to be knit (shown in illustration). For a purl row, insert crochet hook, from back to front into stitch, catching next horizontal yarn "ladder rung" and drawing it through stitch on hook.

Matching method to knit and purl, work up each rung until you reach the row you are working on.

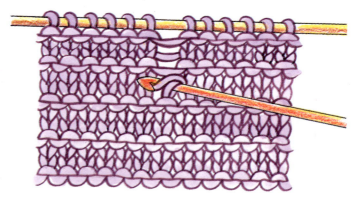

# correcting mistakes

## ■ a dropped purl stitch

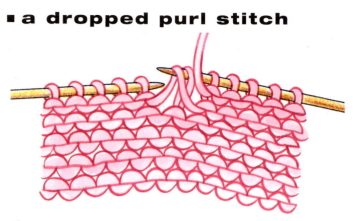

1 Insert right needle, from back to front, first into stitch below and then under yarn of dropped stitch.

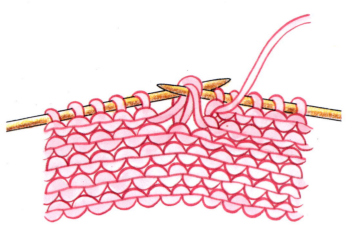

2 Insert left needle into picked-up stitch from the back (as shown) and pull it upward and in front.

3 Then withdraw right needle tip, bringing yarn of dropped stitch through picked-up stitch to restore dropped stitch to needle.

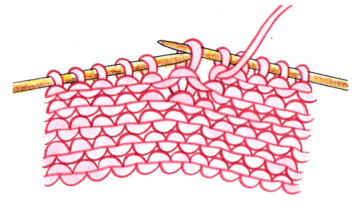

4 Transfer restored stitch from right needle to left needle, sliding off picked-up stitch; proceed with your work normally.

## ■ error in stockinette stitch pattern

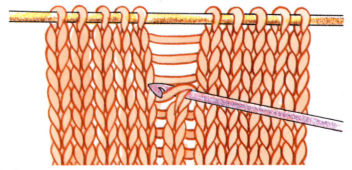

1 Undo corresponding stitches above error until you reach row with error; undo error. Working on knit side, insert crochet hook into front of stitch just below; catch horizontal yarn "ladder rung" and draw it through stitch on hook to restore stitch. In this manner, work up each rung in order until you reach top row.

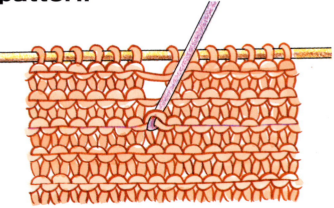

2 If the stitch you need to pick up is on purl side, insert crochet hook from back to front to draw yarn rung through stitch on hook. Work up rungs to top. You can also turn work and work from knit side, if you prefer.

# finishing

**B**efore completing a garment, you may wish to prepare the various pattern pieces, straighten the curled up edges, and at the same time straighten any irregularity of the stitches. This procedure is called blocking and can be done with water or, in some cases, steam.

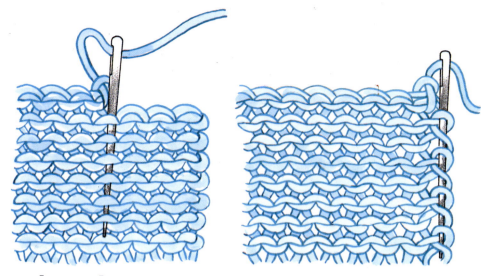

## ■ how to prepare your work

Before blocking, weave in all yarn ends on each piece. With a yarn needle, weave them into stitches on wrong side or along edges (as shown).

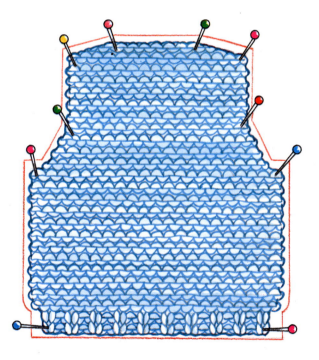

## ■ shaping with steam

Use for wool yarns, but check yarn label first before steaming. Lay an actual-size cardboard pattern piece on a flat surface. Place corresponding knitted piece over it, wrong side up. Using rustproof pins, carefully pin corners and wherever else you find it necessary to keep edges flat. Pass a steaming iron over it, keeping it slightly lifted so that you dampen whole piece evenly. Let piece dry completely before removing pins.

## ■ shaping with water

If the garment is worked with a textured pattern, avoid using an iron for shaping. Mount each piece over its cardboard pattern and dampen it with a spray bottle. Let piece dry completely. You can also dampen pieces by leaving them between layers of damp fabric, placed on a flat surface.

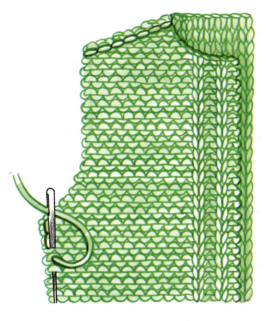

## ▪ how to join the various pieces

**1** With right sides together, join front and back at shoulders and along sides (underarm), sewing edges together with backstitch or other stitch (see page 72).

Sew pieces with same yarn used for knitting garment. (If yarn used is too thick for sewing, use a thinner one, carefully matching colors and fiber content.)

**2** With right sides together, sew underarm seam on sleeve. Turn sleeve right-side out and fold it in half lengthwise, as shown. Mark center of top edge with pin.

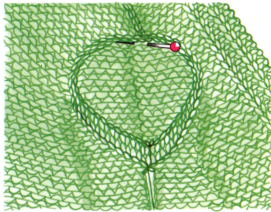

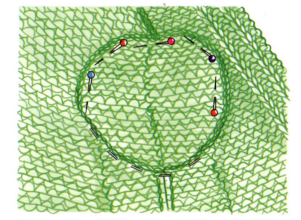

**3** With right sides together, pin sleeve to armhole, matching marked center of sleeve top to shoulder seam and align underarm seams of sleeve and garment body.

**4** Starting at shoulder, pin sleeve edge to armhole, easing and gently curving top of sleeve as shown to fit smoothly. Sew sleeve in place with backstitch.

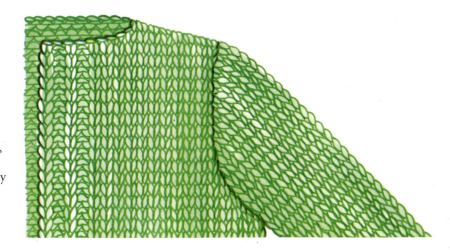

**5** If you can iron the yarn (check label first), keep garment inside out and press edges with tip of iron; turn it right-side out and gently press sewn edge.

# sewing

For a garment to be attractively finished, it is important that the sewing be carefully done. There are different ways of sewing. In all cases, sew just loosely enough that your knitting does not lose its elasticity.

## Invisible Sewing or Horizontal Needle Stitch in a Knit

Stitches to be joined should be placed opposite each other on separate needles, one with right side (front) of work toward you (shown as lower needle) but with the upper needle actually held behind, wrong side toward you (illustration shows them spread for clarity). Thread yarn from back (upper) section in a yarn needle.

**1** Insert yarn needle from front through first stitch on lower needle; * work next 2 stitches above as follows: Pass yarn needle from front (knit side of work) through first stitch and drop it from needle, then pass from back through next stitch and retain it on knitting needle.

**2** Now work 2 lower stitches, passing yarn needle from front through first stitch and drop it, then pass from back through next stitch. Drop each stitch off needle only after it is worked twice. Repeat from * across. Pull yarn just tightly enough for sewn stitches to match knitted ones.

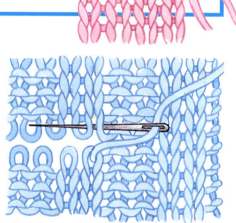

**1** **Invisible Sewing on Stitches in a Purl**
This technique is worked in just the reverse of knit one.

Begin with 1 stitch, then alternating up and down, work 2 stitches each side, working the first stitch from back and the next one from front.

**2** **Invisible Sewing on Garter Stitch**
Position work so that back needle (top edge in illustration) has 2 rows of stitch loops showing beyond ridge and front (lower edge) has 1 row of loops showing above ridge. Insert yarn needle into first stitch on top as if to knit, then * work first lower stitch in a knit (drop it from needle) and the next in a purl; work first top stitch again in a purl (drop it) and next in a knit. Repeat from * across, being careful not to twist stitches as you work them.

▼

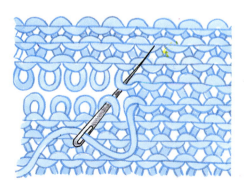

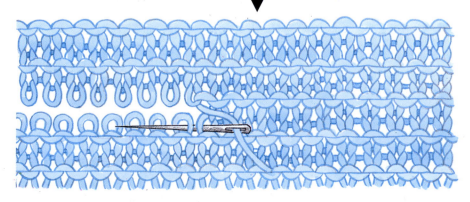

**3** **Invisible Sewing in K2, P2 Ribbing**
Combine the 2 techniques of invisible sewing on knits and on purls in order to work stitches without twisting them.
**NOTE:** This type of sewing can be done only if stitches are knitted in same direction; undo beginning row on top section.

# sewing

**4** **Sewing in Slipstitch**
This is a common stitch used for most types of regular edges. Use same yarn used for garment, unless it is too thick; in which case, use a thinner yarn, matching color and fiber to garment.

Join 2 edges from wrong side, working into back of stitches near or at edges (as shown). Draw 2 edges firmly, but not too tightly, together.

**5** **Sewing in Backstitch**
Use this stitch for joining irregular edges caused by shaping, such as attaching sleeves to armholes.

Hold pieces with right sides together. Sew seam close to edge with backstitch as follows: Sew each stitch, going in a small space to the right, and emerging at a small space to the left, of where yarn originally emerged.

**6** **Sewing in Crossed Stitch**
This is a decorative stitch worked on the right side of your work in contrasting shade. Stitch first in one direction, then back in opposite direction, working even stitches in both directions.

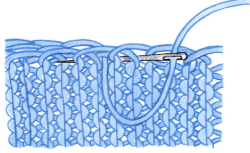

**7** **Sewing in Vertical Knit Stitch**
Holding 2 edges butted together, with right sides toward you, line up first 2 stitches, then * insert yarn needle through center of corresponding end stitch on each edge, as shown.

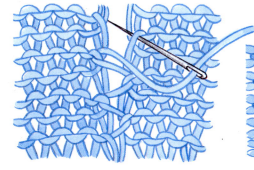

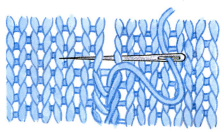

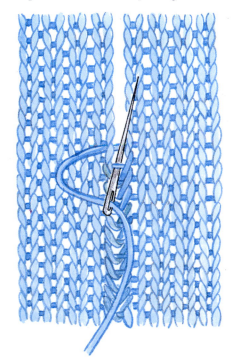

Take needle to back under horizontal yarn of previous stitch and bring it back to front through new stitch just made. Repeat from * to work joining.

---

## Edges Crocheted with Single Crochet Stitch

Hold two pieces with right sides together. Using yarn used for garment, form a loop on hook. With yarn at back of work, * insert hook through corresponding stitches of both pieces, catch a loop of yarn on hook and draw through both pieces. Reach back, catch another loop on hook (edges are wrapped within crochet), and draw this loop through the 2 loops on hook. Repeat from * across edge.

## Free Stitches Connected by Crochet Hook

Lay 2 pieces flat with right-sides up and free-stitch edges butted together. With crochet hook, pick up first stitch on right piece, * then pick up corresponding stitch on left piece and draw it though stitch on hook; pick up next stitch on right and draw it through; repeat from * to join edges. Secure last stitch.

Work on right side for decorative seam and on wrong side for invisible seam.

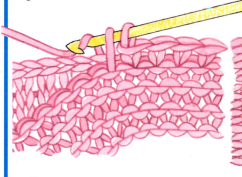

# buttonholes and loops

Vertical or horizontal buttonholes are worked as you knit and require precision in your finishing. The button loops are done at the end of your work on the borders along the edges.

### ■ simple horizontal buttonhole

**1** To work buttonhole at desired place, bind off enough stitches, without knitting them, to accommodate button. On left needle, pick up last remaining stitch from binding off and proceed as usual with your work.

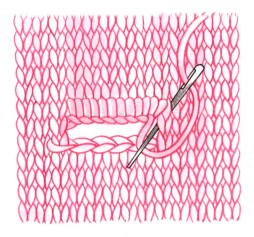

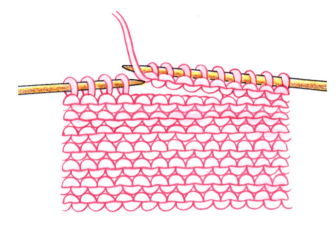

**2** On next row over buttonhole, cast on as many stitches as were bound off: Turn work and cast on with 2 needles (see page 9). Turn work again to complete row.

**3** When garment is completed, finish buttonhole edges by embroidering in buttonhole stitch (see diagram) with same yarn as garment or with silk yarn in same color.

## Horizontal Buttonhole Worked on only 1 Row

**1** Bind off desired stitches for buttonhole, without knitting them, using crochet hook. Place remaining stitch on hook onto left needle.

**2** Cast on as many stitches as were bound off, working them onto right needle with single needle (see page 15), then complete row.

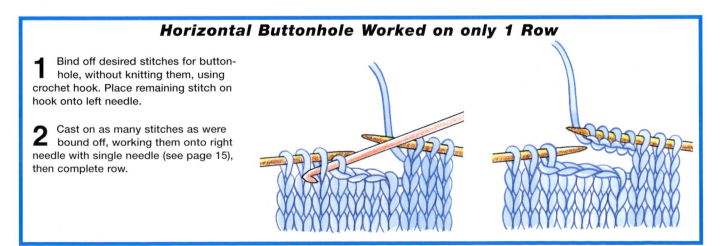

# buttonholes and loops

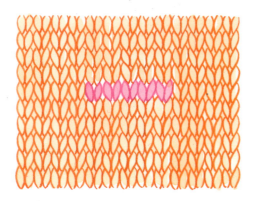

## ■ tailor's buttonhole

**1** At the place desired for buttonhole, use contrasting color yarn to knit the number of stitches needed for buttonhole. Slide these stitches back onto left needle and knit them again with main color yarn.

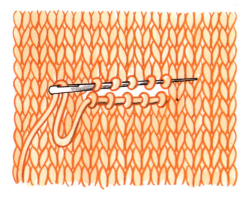

**2** When work is completed, remove colored yarn and sew a yarn strand through them to prevent their unraveling.

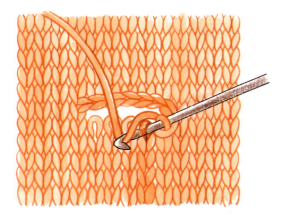

**3** Finish buttonhole with a discreet stitch as follows: With yarn at back of work, use crochet hook to bind off stitches, as shown, around buttonhole. Buttonhole stitch can also be used to finish buttonhole.

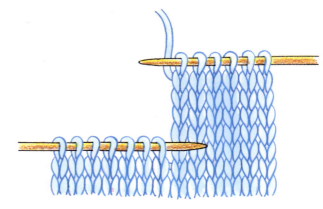

## ■ vertical buttonhole

**1** Divide work at the point where you plan to make buttonhole and work the 2 sides separately. First work right side to desired length of buttonhole.

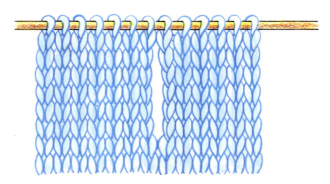

**2** Work second side to correspond. Then continue to work across both sections as usual, connecting the 2 parts. Embroider edges of buttonhole with buttonhole stitch.

### Button Loop

Work button loop on outside edge once you have finished work. At place for button loop, attach yarn and sew a loop of 2 or 3 strands at edge, as shown, making loop big enough for button. Cover strands with buttonhole stitch.

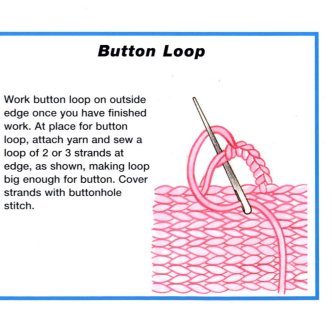

# pockets 1

In addition to their use in holding things, pockets can be decorative. They are made in different ways. Choose the one most suitable for the garment you want to make.

## ■ internal pocket with border

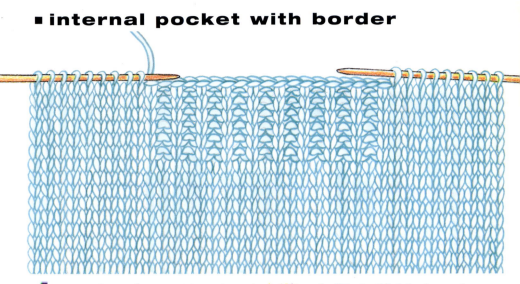

**1** Work front of garment to within 1 inch (2½ cm) of desired height for pocket opening. Mark beginning and end of opening at desired position, then continue with your work, knitting pocket stitches between markers in k1, p1 ribbing stitch and remaining stitches as before.

Once you have finished edge (1 inch/2½ cm high), bind off pocket stitches on a right side row and complete row.

**2** On separate needle, cast on same number of stitches as for pocket, plus 2 extra stitches for each selvage. Knit in stockinette stitch to almost same length as front to pocket opening, ending with knit row and binding off 2 selvage stitches on each side on last row. Place these stitches on a holder for pocket lining and cut yarn.

Beginning with purl row, work front stitches to pocket opening, purl pocket lining stitches off holder, then continue working remaining front stitches to end of row. Now you should have the same number of stitches on needle as you began with.

**3** Proceed as usual with your work. When garment is finished, sew the 3 sides of the pocket lining to the back with little hidden stitches.

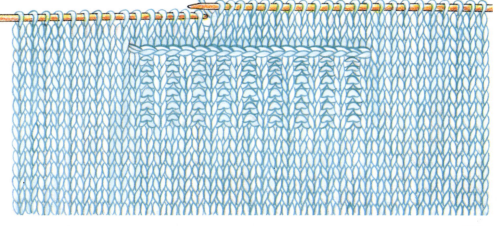

# pockets 1

**■ vertical pocket with picked up edge**

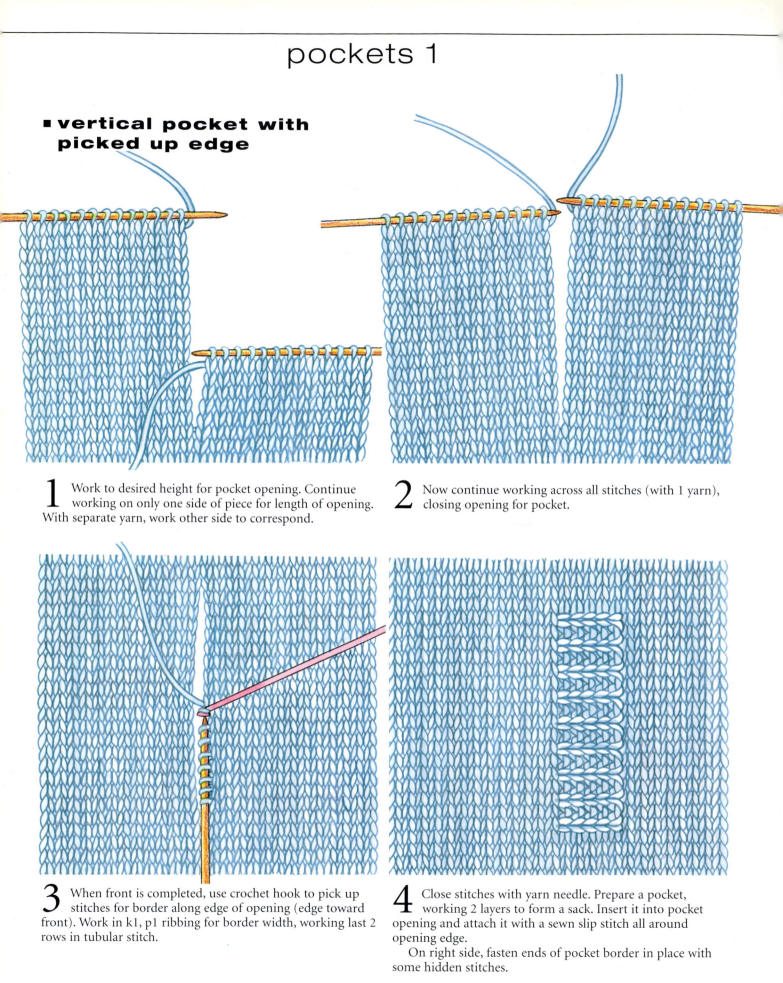

**1** Work to desired height for pocket opening. Continue working on only one side of piece for length of opening. With separate yarn, work other side to correspond.

**2** Now continue working across all stitches (with 1 yarn), closing opening for pocket.

**3** When front is completed, use crochet hook to pick up stitches for border along edge of opening (edge toward front). Work in k1, p1 ribbing for border width, working last 2 rows in tubular stitch.

**4** Close stitches with yarn needle. Prepare a pocket, working 2 layers to form a sack. Insert it into pocket opening and attach it with a sewn slip stitch all around opening edge.

On right side, fasten ends of pocket border in place with some hidden stitches.

# pockets 2

**■ slanting pocket with picked up edge**

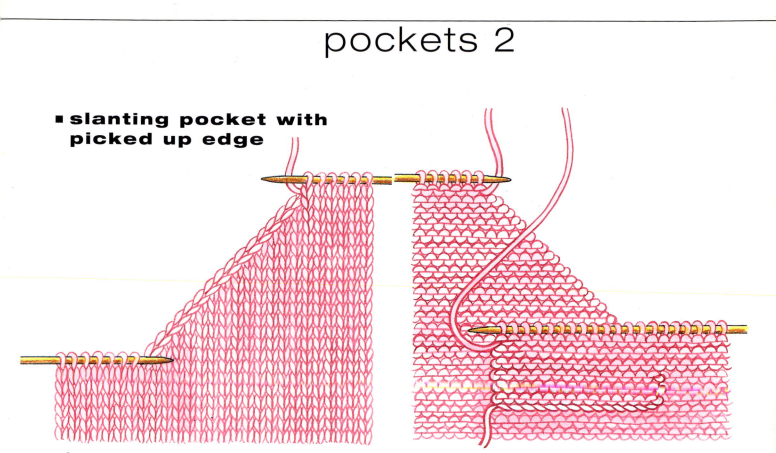

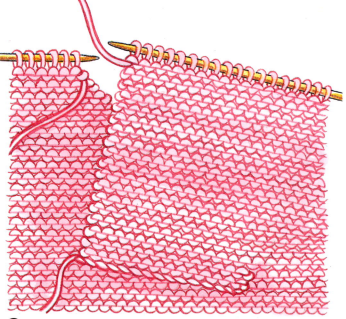

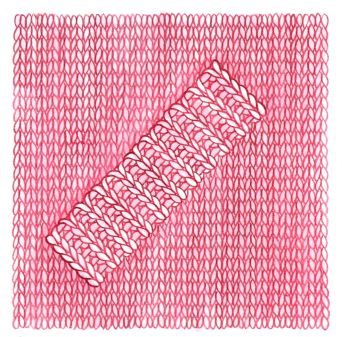

**1** Work piece to desired height for pocket opening. Divide work into 2 parts, one for front edge and pocket and the remaining stitches placed on a holder. Continue to work front edge and pocket stitches. At pocket edge, start shaping pocket opening by decreasing 1 or 2 stitches (depending on slant desired) every other row. When all pocket opening stitches are decreased, set remaining stitches aside.

**2** To make the pocket lining, cast on enough stitches to equal pocket decreases on a new needle. Work pocket lining in stockinette stitch for 2 inches (5 cm), then add to needle those stitches left unworked at start of pocket opening. Continue working on all of these stitches.

**3** When this part measures same as other part to top of pocket opening, add to needle the remaining stitches (at front of pocket), pushing them close to stitches you are working on; continue to work as usual on all stitches and complete front.

**4** When garment is completed, pick up stitches along pocket opening and work k1, p1 ribbing for depth desired, working last 3 or 4 rows in tubular stitches. Close edge with yarn needle. Attach ribbing ends in place with small hidden stitches. On wrong side, attach pocket lining to garment with a few hidden stitches.

# pockets 2

## ■ sewn on pocket with knitted edge

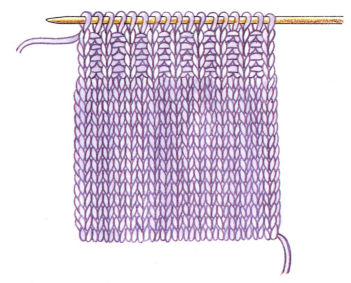

**1** Cast on 2 stitches fewer than needed for desired width. Purl first row, then continue in stockinette stitch, increasing 1 stitch at each end of first 3 rows (adding 6 stitches in all).

When pocket is desired length, bind off 2 stitches on each side, and, with larger needles, work in k1, p1 ribbing for 1 inch (2½ cm). Finish edge with 3 or 4 rows in tubular stitch; close stitches with yarn needle.

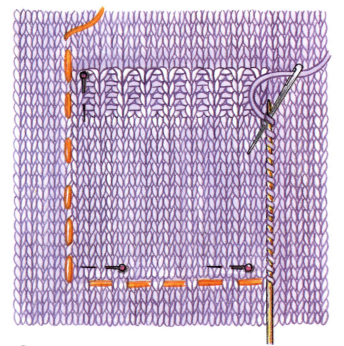

**2** Fold under added stitches on sides of pocket and at bottom; sew them in place.

Pin pocket to garment. To facilitate sewing, use a knitting needle to pick up stitches of garment along edge and sew each picked-up stitch to corresponding stitch of pocket.

## Sewn On Pocket on Picked Up Stitches

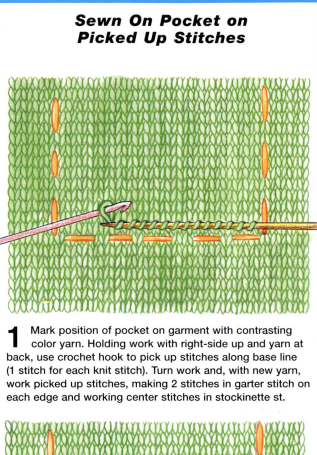

**1** Mark position of pocket on garment with contrasting color yarn. Holding work with right-side up and yarn at back, use crochet hook to pick up stitches along base line (1 stitch for each knit stitch). Turn work and, with new yarn, work picked up stitches, making 2 stitches in garter stitch on each edge and working center stitches in stockinette st.

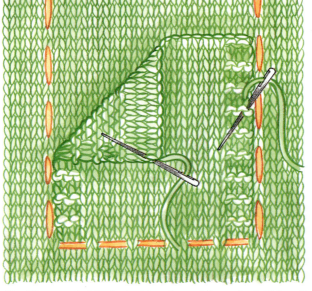

**2** When pocket is desired length, purl 1 row for fold line. For hem, use smaller needles to work 4 rows in stockinette stitch, decreasing 1 stitch at each side of first row. Bind off.

Fold hem under and sew it in place with slip stitches; sew sides of pocket in place.

# elastic band edges

## ■ herringbone stitch band

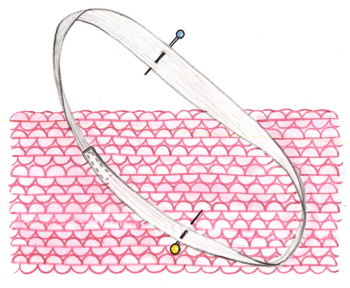

**1** Cut elastic to desired measurement, adding an extra inch (2½ cm) for overlapping ends to form circle; stitch ends securely together.

**2** Position elastic band, on wrong side, around waist edge, and pin it, evenly distributing it.

**3** Using thick embroidery yarn in same shade as garment, insert needle from right to left, picking up 2 stitches just above elastic band.

**4** Move needle down and to the right to pick up 2 stitches below elastic band.

**5** Continue in this manner, inserting needle below, then above elastic band, always working to the right of previous stitch to form casing for elastic band until you have worked all the way around.

# elastic band edges

## ■ crocheted band

◆ Prepare elastic band and pin it to waist edge (see previous page).

◆ Crochet long strand worked in chain stitch, making it about three times waist measurement and leaving yarn attached to add more if needed.

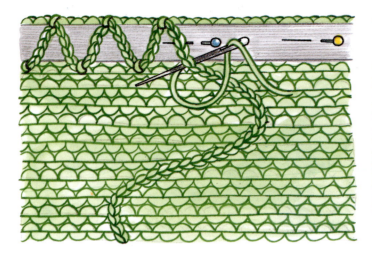

**1** Stitch 1 end of strand above elastic band. Bring it down and to right, and stitch it below elastic.

**2** Continue in this manner, stitching strand first above, then below, forming a zigzag pattern.

### Edge with Elastic Inserted on Back of Stitches

To get more hold along edges (such as for a beret or a pair of socks), add elastic to your work. The knitting methods are illustrated below.

Knit edge, with elastic held at back of work and catching it in work as if it were a second color (see jacquard stitch, page 102).

You can also add elastic to completed ribbed edge, using a tapestry needle on back to pass needle under vertical knit stitches on each row of edge.

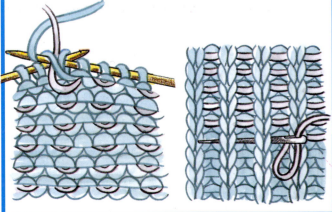

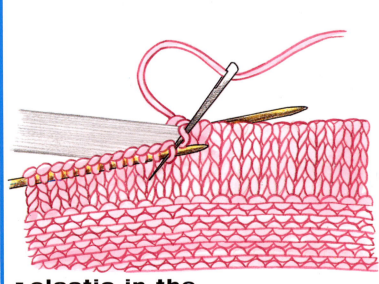

## ■ elastic in the tubular edge

Make an edge in tubular stitch, working to desired height. Divide stitches onto 2 needles. Insert elastic band (see previous page), and close edge (see page 21), concealing elastic within casing.

# mending, reinforcing, patching

**E**ven a hand-knit garment can be damaged or have a hole at some point. This is why it is essential to know the best way to repair the damage before it gets worse.

## ■ mending

Holes in stockinette stitch can be repaired with invisible mending that reconstructs the stitches.

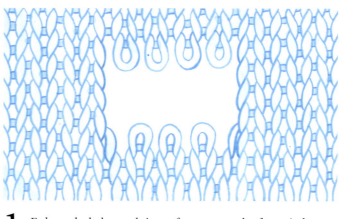

**1** Enlarge hole by undoing a few rows and a few stitches to form a square.

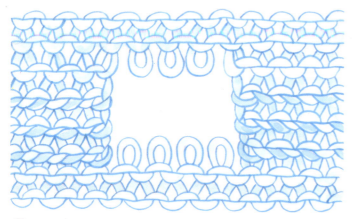

**2** Secure yarn ends on wrong side, weaving them into stitches with yarn needle. Pin work area with hole to piece of cardboard to keep it stretched.

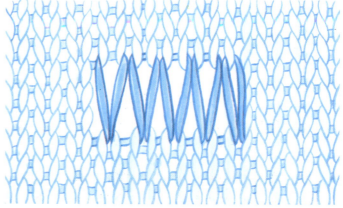

**3** With yarn, work large vertical stitches (as shown) from lower edge stitches to corresponding upper edge stitches, passing yarn twice through each stitch.

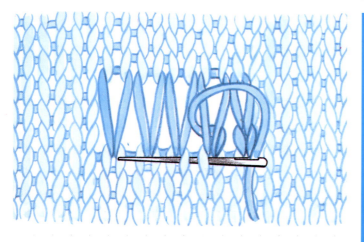

**4** Reconstruct stitches, a row at a time, by working from right to left and making each stitch around 2 vertical strands. At side edges of hole, catch half stitches (as at right edge in illustration) in repair stitch, and attach to back of loop when there is a whole stitch (as at left). At end of row, turn work and work back in purl stitches.

## Reinforcing in Knit Stitch

Use this for repairing stitches where the yarn has worn thin and is in danger of breaking. Work same as for embroidering duplicate stitch (see page 129), turning work around at beginning of each row and using thinner yarn of matching color (untwist original yarn, separating plies).

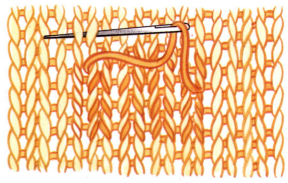

# mending, reinforcing, patching

## ■ the patch

If the hole is large, you need to rework whole section. Enlarge hole into square as previously explained and, on back of work, attach yarn at lower corner.

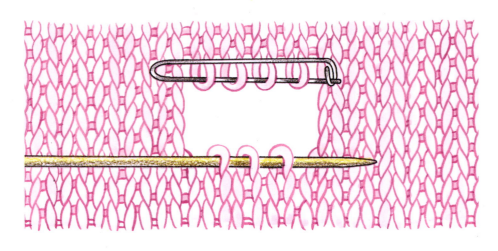

**1** Place top edge stitches on a holder; place lower edge stitches on a knitting needle.

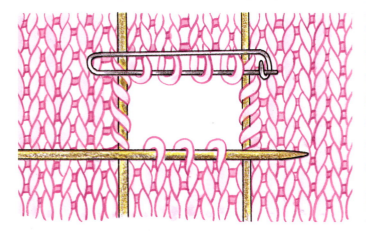

**2** With 2 other needles, pick up side edge stitches as shown. Starting from bottom, knit missing section, working back and forth in rows and, at end of each row, knit together last stitch on needle and corresponding stitch on main section.

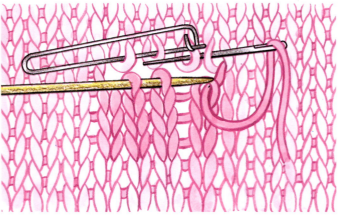

**3** Connect patch to top stitches, sewing them 1 by 1 in knit stitch (as shown) with a yarn needle.

### Mending On Knits with Horizontal Yarns

This is another way of mending that is less precise than that explained on previous page. Prepare section to be repaired as described. Then stitch the supporting yarns horizontally, anchoring them 1 stitch from edge. Pin to cardboard, then reconstruct stitches vertically, knitting over each supporting yarn. Work full stitch over half-stitch at edge (shown at left edge).

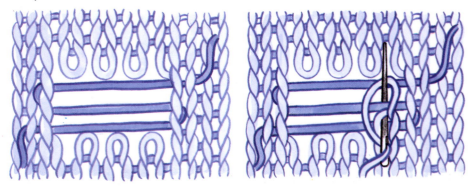

# horizontal darts

Even in knitting you sometimes need to make darts, either vertical or horizontal, for extra fullness and a better-fitting garment. They are made by using special techniques as you knit the piece.

The horizontal darts are worked in short rows where you knit only partway across the row before turning to work back to the beginning. First, determine the number of stitches needed for the dart. Divide this number by 4, 5, or 6 to find the number of stitches to set aside on each short row.

**NOTE:** The higher the divisor, the larger (deeper) the dart will be.

## ■ horizontal dart on the right side

**1** On first row of dart, knit across to last few stitches and set aside these stitches without knitting them.

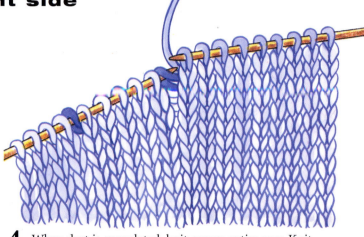

**4** When dart is completed, knit across entire row. Knit together as one each pair of yo and slip stitches.

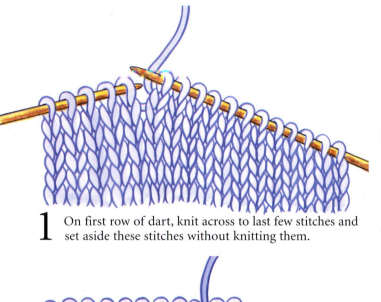

**2** Turn work, make yarn over (yo) stitch, then slip first stitch onto right needle; purl remaining stitches.

**3** Continue on short rows. Set aside new group of stitches each knit row, work yo, and slip 1 to start each purl row.

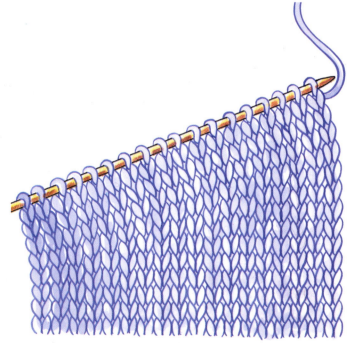

**5** This is how the completed right dart should look.

# horizontal darts

## ■ horizontal dart on the left side

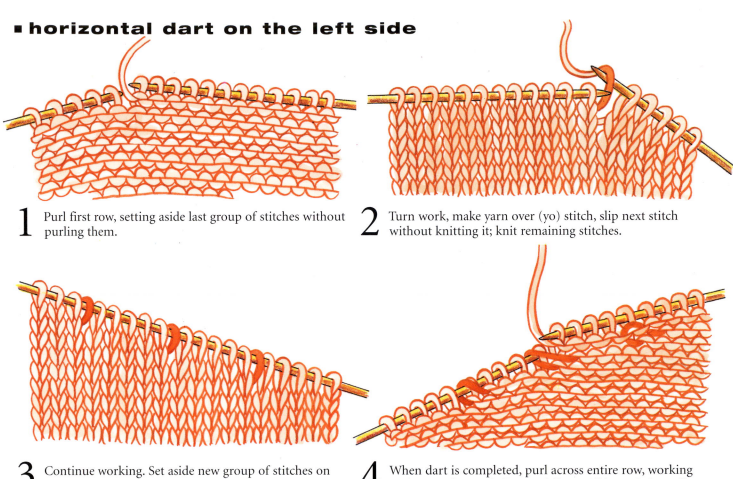

1 Purl first row, setting aside last group of stitches without purling them.

2 Turn work, make yarn over (yo) stitch, slip next stitch without knitting it; knit remaining stitches.

3 Continue working. Set aside new group of stitches on each purl row, work yo, and slip 1 to start each knit row.

4 When dart is completed, purl across entire row, working each pair of yo and slip 1 as follows: Slide 2 stitches off left needle to interchange their positions so slip stitch comes before yo; return to left needle and purl them together as one.

### TIPS

Home-washed sweaters may felt and curl up if you don't follow the following rules:

- Always use lukewarm water in washing and rinsing.

- The detergent should be one suitable for wool, not regular powder.

- Don't soak the garment for too long.

- When washing it, don't rub. Gently squeeze it with your hands.

- Eliminate as much water as possible without twisting or wringing, but by rolling sweater in a soft towel.

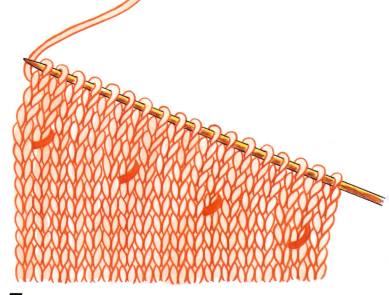

5 This is how the completed left dart should look.

# vertical darts

## ▪ vertical darts

Vertical darts are made with a series of decreases and increases. To make a skirt, it is enough to make decreases from the hip to the waistline. On a dress, however, you need to make the decreases on the skirt, but on the bodice, from the waistline to the bust, you need to make increases.

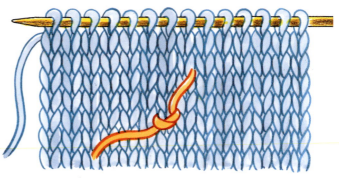

1 Establish position for darts, and mark, with contrasting color yarn, a stitch for center of each dart.

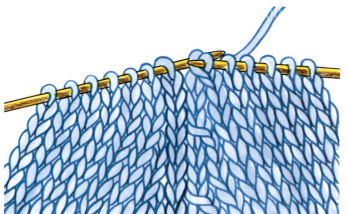

2 Make a decrease before marked center as follows: On 2 stitches just before center, slip 1 stitch without knitting, knit next stitch, pass slipped stitch over knit, and drop it (decrease made before center).

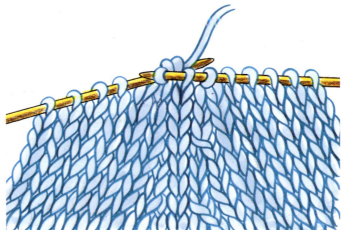

3 Knit center stitch, then knit next 2 stitches together as one (decrease made after center stitch). Continuing in same manner, decrease at regular intervals (illustration shows every 4th row) to waistline. At this point, begin bodice darts.

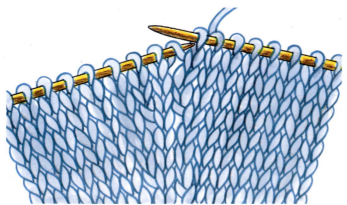

4 Keeping same center stitch, increase at regular intervals at center stitch as follows: Knit to center stitch, then, with tip of right needle, pick up horizontal yarn connecting last stitch to center and place this loop on left needle; knit new stitch in a twist; knit center stitch, then increase as before just after center.

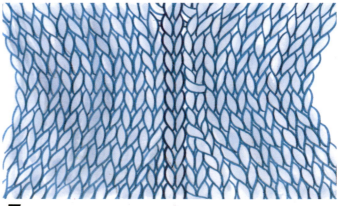

5 Continue in this manner until dart is completed.

# vertical darts

## Vertical Dart from the Right

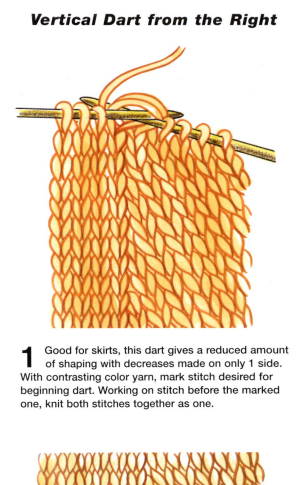

**1** Good for skirts, this dart gives a reduced amount of shaping with decreases made on only 1 side. With contrasting color yarn, mark stitch desired for beginning dart. Working on stitch before the marked one, knit both stitches together as one.

**2** Repeat this decrease every 4 or 6 rows (knit rows), depending on how big you want the dart to be until you have enough decreases.

## Waistline Dart

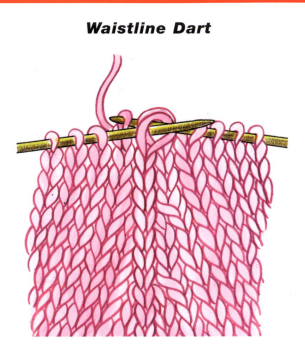

**1** With contrasting color yarn, mark center stitch desired for beginning dart. Work double decrease as follows: Work to last stitch before the marked one, slip next 2 stitches (as if to knit them together) onto right needle without actually knitting them, knit next stitch, and pass the 2 slipped stitches over the one just knitted.

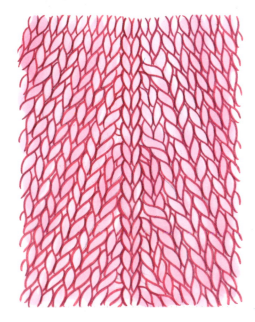

**2** Repeat this decrease every 2 or 4 rows, depending on how big you want the dart to be until you have enough decreases.

# tucks

## ■ how to make horizontal tucks

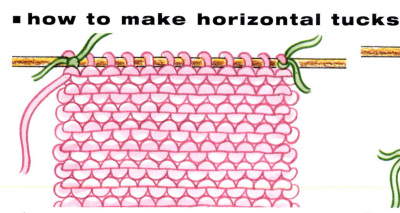

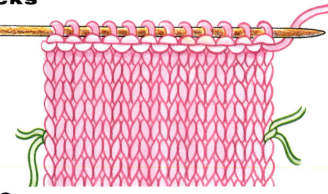

**1** Knit in stockinette stitch to desired row for tuck, ending with purl row. With contrasting color yarn, mark 2 end stitches of last row. Continue to work until you have worked (above markers) half the number of rows desired for the tuck (5 rows shown), ending with a knit row.

**2** Knit a row to mark the fold line of the tuck. A ridge appears on the front of your work.

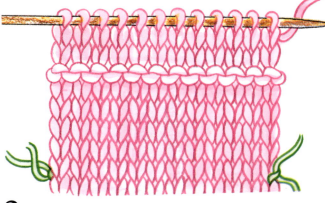

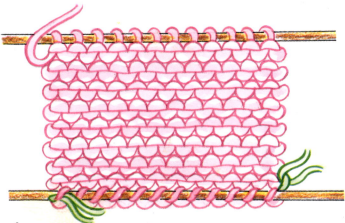

**3** Work second half of tuck, starting with knit row, until you have 1 row fewer than first half, ending with purl row.

**4** On wrong side of work, use knitting needle to pick up stitches belonging to marked row, picking up as many stitches as were initially cast on.

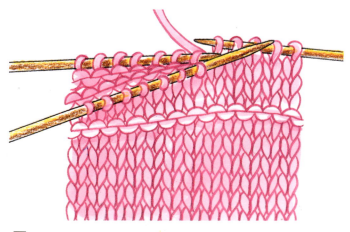

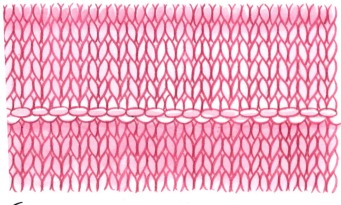

**5** On right side of work, join edges as follows: Keeping stitch holder behind your work, knit together stitch from knitting needle with corresponding stitch from stitch holder.

**6** Continue knitting the garment up to next tuck.

# tucks

## Tuck with Cat's Tooth Edge

To make pleat with decorative edge, mark fold line with row of small eyelets. Work half of tuck, then, instead of ridge, work as follows: * Purl 1 stitch and slip it back to left needle, pass next stitch over purl stitch and drop, slip purl stitch back to right needle, make yarn over; repeat from * across, ending with purl stitch. Complete tuck, which will have lacy edge called "cat's tooth."

## Curved Tuck

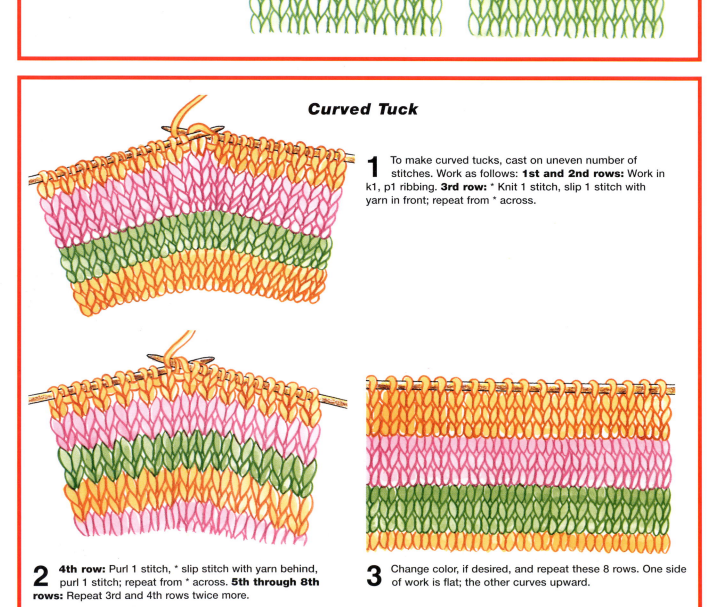

**1** To make curved tucks, cast on uneven number of stitches. Work as follows: **1st and 2nd rows:** Work in k1, p1 ribbing. **3rd row:** * Knit 1 stitch, slip 1 stitch with yarn in front; repeat from * across.

**2** **4th row:** Purl 1 stitch, * slip stitch with yarn behind, purl 1 stitch; repeat from * across. **5th through 8th rows:** Repeat 3rd and 4th rows twice more.

**3** Change color, if desired, and repeat these 8 rows. One side of work is flat; the other curves upward.

# pleats

**P**leats can be used for knitting skirts. They can be flat pleats, box pleats, and plissé. For all of them, use a thin yarn so garment does not become too bulky.

Determine the number of stitches needed for the width of the garment plus total number of stitches needed for under layers of each pleat. When you work, mark separation between 1 pleat and next by slipping 1 stitch (outer fold line) and mark depth of pleat with 1 purl stitch (inner fold line). In example shown here: * Knit 8 stitches, slip 1, knit 4, purl 1; repeat from * across, ending knit 8 stitches. On wrong side rows, purl stitches, but knit inner fold stitches.

### ▪ flat pleat

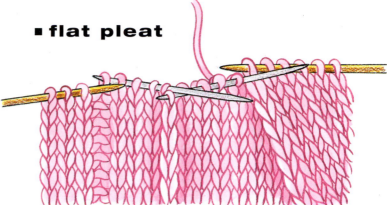

**1** Work to desired length for folding and closing pleats, knit 4 then put next 4 stitches and slip stitch on a double pointed (dp) needle; put next 4 stitches and purl 1 on another dp needle; keep last 8 stitches on left needle.

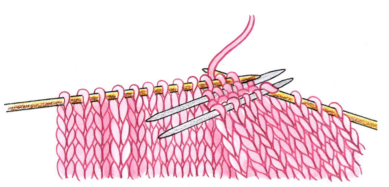

**2** Fold second dp needle (4 stitches and purl 1) to back, holding it (wrong sides together) behind first dp needle. Now * knit 3 stitches together, working through first stitch on each dp needle and left needle; repeat from * 4 times more.

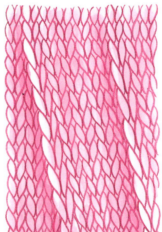

**3** Repeat this process until you have formed all the pleats, then continue to work in regular stockinette stitch on all stitches.

### ▪ box pleat

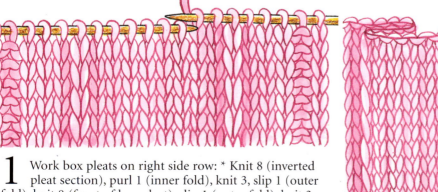

**1** Work box pleats on right side row: * Knit 8 (inverted pleat section), purl 1 (inner fold), knit 3, slip 1 (outer fold), knit 8 (front of box pleat), slip 1 (outer fold), knit 3, purl 1 (inner fold); repeat from * across, ending with knit 8.

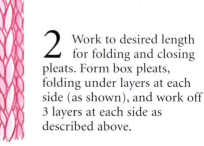

**2** Work to desired length for folding and closing pleats. Form box pleats, folding under layers at each side (as shown), and work off 3 layers at each side as described above.

# pleats

## ▪ plissé pleats

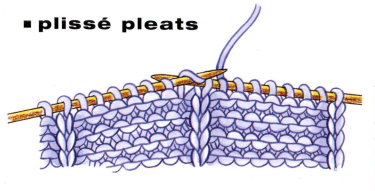

1 To work plissé pleats, cast on a number of stitches in multiples of 8. On right side rows, * knit 7, purl 1; repeat from * across. On wrong side rows, knit 4, * purl 1, knit 7; repeat from * across, ending with knit 3.

2 Work to length desired and complete piece. The garment should exhibit typical look of plissé pleats.

---

### Curve with Decreases

To draw in work with a gentle curve, be sure to distribute decreases at regular intervals.

For each decrease, knit 2 stitches together as one. The more decreases, the greater the curve; the fewer decreases, the less the curve.

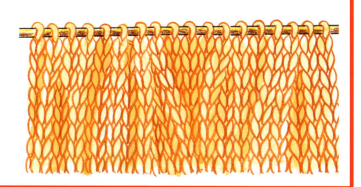

---

### Curve with Increases

To enlarge work with a curve, be sure to distribute increases at regular intervals. For each increase, knit same stitch with 1 regular knit (in front loop) and 1 twisted knit (in back loop). The fullness of curve depends on number of stitches increased and how closely spaced they are. For very full curve (as shown), increase in each stitch; for less fullness, space increases farther apart.

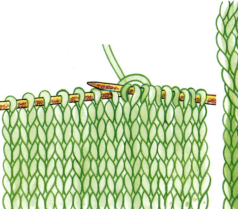

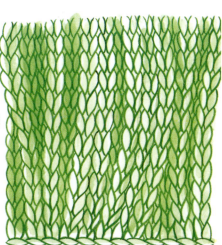

# elaborate cable stitch

Always popular, cables can be made in many different ways. Knitting them with a large number of stitches will give you a fuller and more intricate cable.

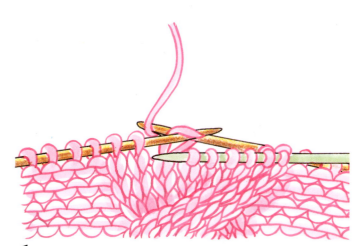

**1** This cable is worked in stockinette stitch on 9 stitches. Knit desired number of rows to cable twist. Work twist as follows: Slip first 6 stitches to cable needle, or double pointed (dp) needle, and hold in front of work; knit last 3 cable stitches.

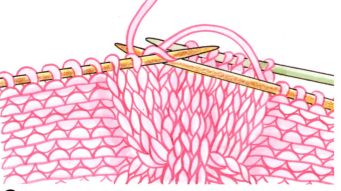

**2** Return 4th, 5th, and 6th stitches to left needle and move first 3 cable stitches still on dp needle to back of work. Knit 3 stitches on left needle, then stitches from dp needle.

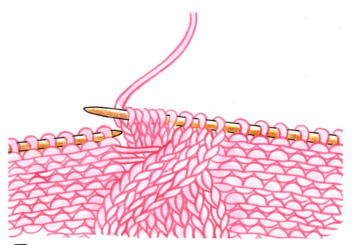

**3** Now continue in stockinette stitch to next cable twist. Slip first 6 stitches to dp needle and hold at back; knit next 3 stitches.

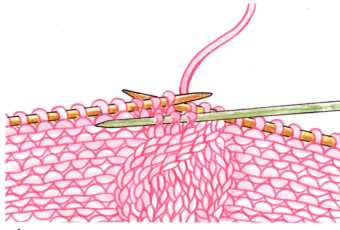

**4** Place 4th, 5th, and 6th stitches back onto left needle; bring 3 stitches on dp needle to front of work.

**5** Return 3 stitches on dp needle to left needle before 4th, 5th, and 6th stitches; knit all 6 stitches.

# elaborate cable stitch

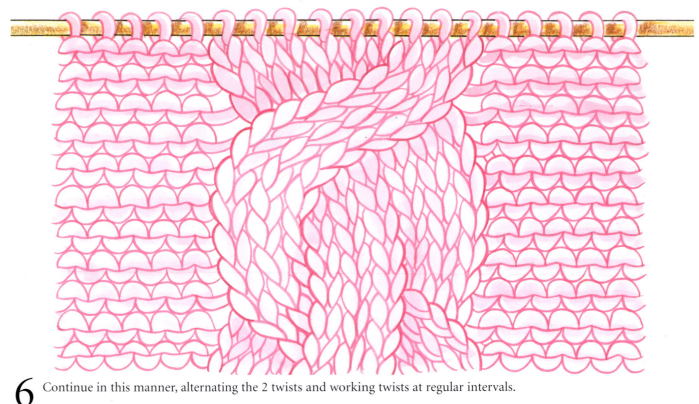

**6** Continue in this manner, alternating the 2 twists and working twists at regular intervals.

## Extending Cable Along Neck Opening

With some cables, it is possible to continue them along edges of neck opening by working neck decreases in stitches just next to cable stitches.

In example shown here, double cable is divided into 2 single cables that extend along neck opening.

The neck opening edge is finished by cables, but other finishing can be added, if desired. For instance, when you knit neck cables, you can add a selvage stitch to neck edge of each cable.

# finishing with a crochet hook

**C**rocheted trims are easy and fast to make. They can be used for completing a garment in a decorative manner or for finishing uneven edges. In both cases, you can use contrasting color yarn.

## ■ slip stitch edge

Work right to left on right side of work, crocheting in rounds, or work rows in the same direction, cutting yarn at end of row and starting again at right end. Crochet a slip stitch in back loop of each stitch across. Work 2 or more rows.

## ■ picot trim

**1** This trim is worked in only 1 row, from right to left, as follows: Work single crochet (sc) stitch, working into first stitch along edge, then * make 3 chain (ch) stitches, crochet sc into first (beginning) stitch of chain-3, skip 1 or 2 stitches along edge, crochet another sc in next edge stitch.

**2** Repeat from * along edge, ending with sc. Fasten off.

## ■ shell stitch edge

Work in only 1 row from right to left: In first edge stitch, crochet * 1 single crochet (sc) stitch, 3 chain (ch) stitches, and 3 double crochet (dc) stitches; skip 2 or 3 stitches along the edge; repeat from *.

## ■ reverse single crochet

Crochet a row of single crochet (sc) along knitted edge, spacing stitches to keep edge even and flat. Then, without turning work, crochet from left to right, making sc in each sc of row just completed. Work back to beginning of edging. Fasten off.

# finishing with a crochet hook

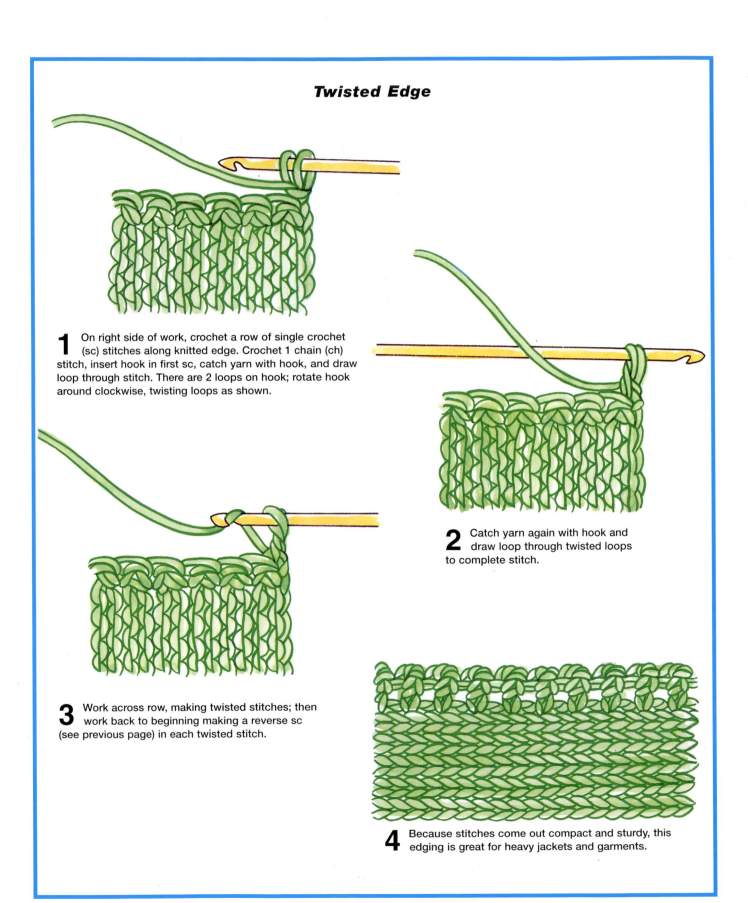

### Twisted Edge

**1** On right side of work, crochet a row of single crochet (sc) stitches along knitted edge. Crochet 1 chain (ch) stitch, insert hook in first sc, catch yarn with hook, and draw loop through stitch. There are 2 loops on hook; rotate hook around clockwise, twisting loops as shown.

**2** Catch yarn again with hook and draw loop through twisted loops to complete stitch.

**3** Work across row, making twisted stitches; then work back to beginning making a reverse sc (see previous page) in each twisted stitch.

**4** Because stitches come out compact and sturdy, this edging is great for heavy jackets and garments.

# shoulder pads

Sometimes a knitted garment requires shoulder pads. It is possible to buy a pair, or you can make them with the same yarn you used for the garment.

## ▪ for light garments

**1** Use the same yarn as for the garment and needles at least 1 size larger. Cast on 3 stitches. Knit in garter stitch, increasing 1 stitch at beginning and end of each row.

**2** Work until piece is 2¾ inches (7 cm) from beginning; work even for ¾ inch (2 cm) more, then decrease 1 stitch at each end of every row.

**3** When there are only 3 stitches left, bind them off loosely.

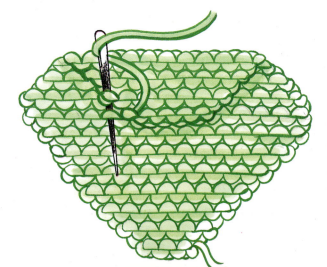

**4** To shape shoulder pad, fold under last decrease row; fold again as shown and sew edges in place with hidden stitches. Make another shoulder pad in same way. Attach inside garment at shoulder so fold is at armhole edge.

# shoulder pads

## ■ for medium to heavy garments

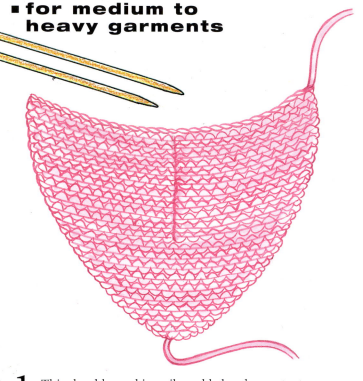

**1** This shoulder pad is easily padded and accentuates shoulders. Use the same yarn as for the garment and large needles to cast on 3 stitches. Knit in garter stitch, increasing 1 stitch at each end on every row. When piece measures 2 inches (5 cm), bind off 2 stitches at center of row every 4th row, continuing to make side increases. When piece measures 4 inches (10 cm), bind off all stitches.

**2** Make another piece the same way. Crochet edges of 2 pieces together with slip stitch, stuffing them if desired before closing them completely. Make second shoulder pad the same way and attach them in place in garment.

## ■ for heavy garments

**1** Use a double strand of same yarn as for the garment and larger needles. Cast on 5 stitches and work in stockinette stitch, increasing 2 stitches on 1st row, 4 stitches on 3rd row, 6 stitches on 5th row. Then knit in garter stitch on center stitches, knitting the first and last 4 stitches in tubular stitch. When piece measures 4 inches (10 cm), bind off 5 stitches on each side and continue working on remaining stitches in garter stitch, for another 2 inches (5 cm). Bind off.

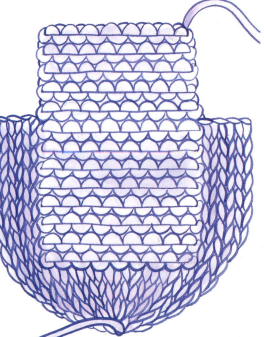

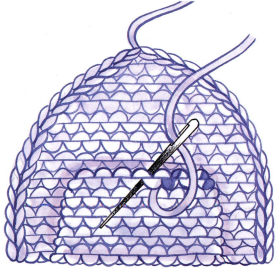

**2** Fold over 2-inch (5-cm) extension on shoulder pad and sew it in place. Make another pad the same way. Attach pads in place inside the garment with folded edge of pad at armhole edge.

# beading 1

**B**eads are often used to turn knitted garments into elegant wear or playful clothes for children. There are beads, sequins, and jewels in many styles, shapes, sizes, and colors available on the market.

■ **how to use beads**

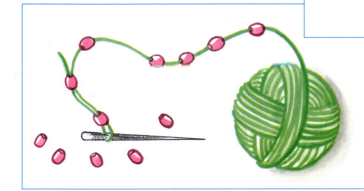

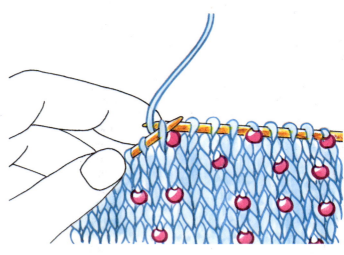

**1** Slide beads onto yarn before beginning work in order to determined how many you will need. If beads have a big hole, thread them directly onto yarn with a needle.

**2** If beads have very small holes, use a very thin needle threaded with a strand of sewing thread. Slide beads onto needle and down thread (looped over yarn as shown); carefully push them past loop and onto yarn.

■ **working without a pattern**

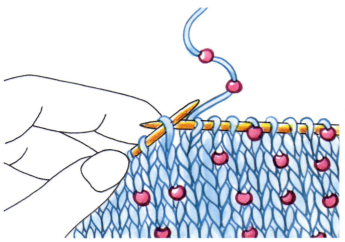

**1** Use beads on a stockinette stitch garment to add texture. To work a bead, on right side row, insert right needle into next stitch through back loop (as if to work a twisted stitch).

**2** Slide bead along yarn to stitch you are knitting and keep it behind this stitch.

# beading 1

**3** Wrap yarn around right needle tip and, with left index finger, push bead between yarn and needle.

**4** Knit stitch and withdraw right needle, slipping bead through stitch and pushing it to front of work.

**5** On wrong side rows, insert right needle into stitch as if to make a twisted purl.

**6** Wrap yarn around right needle tip and slide bead next to stitch.

**7** Complete stitch and withdraw needle, pushing bead to right side of work through finished stitch.

# beading 2

Working with beads is a fun way of personalizing a garment. It is simple and fast, requiring no extra hassle after finishing your work. Instead, the beading "grows" as you knit and is done at the same time your garment is done.

## ■ working with a pattern

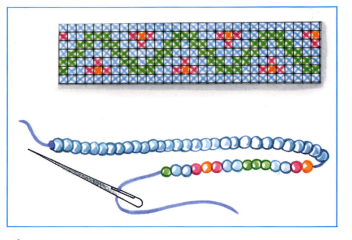

**1** You can follow printed designs, or make your own on graph paper, with each square representing a knit stitch; use colored pencils to indicate the desired colors. If beads are used in a solid pattern, use small beads, such as seed beads, to keep your piece from bunching up. Plan carefully so you can thread beads properly as you need them in your design.

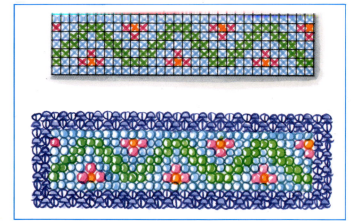

**2** Determine which rows of chart will be knitted and which purled. Thread beads onto needle in order needed as follows: Start at top of chart (first beads threaded are last to be worked) and work down row by row, going from left to right for knit rows and right to left for purl rows. This is the opposite from the way you will read chart to knit actual piece.

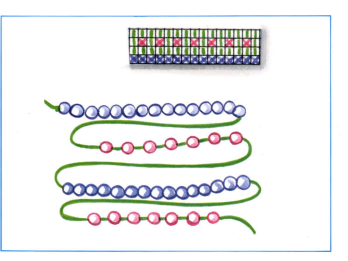

**3** If design is worked only on every other row (usually on right side), you need to thread beads starting from top row and threading left to right for each row.

**4** Beading can be worked in other pattern stitches besides stockinette stitch. Garter stitch, for example, can gain extra color and texture when beads are added.

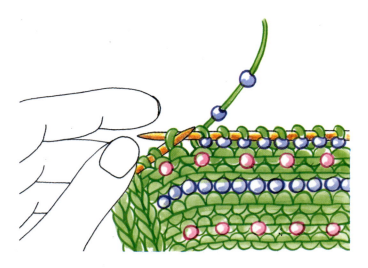

99

# beading 2

## Working with Sequins

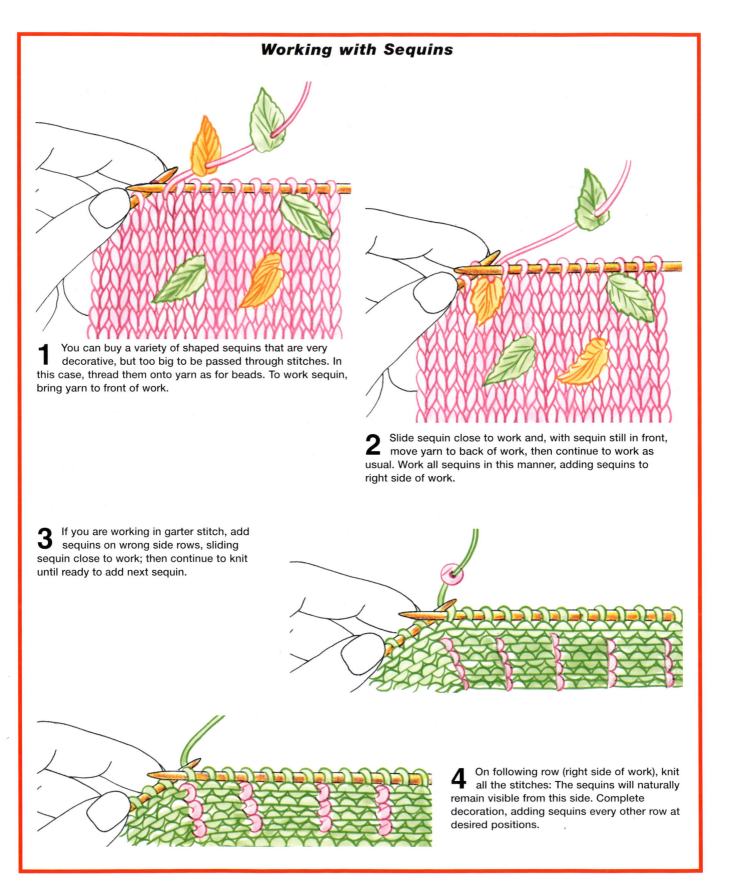

**1** You can buy a variety of shaped sequins that are very decorative, but too big to be passed through stitches. In this case, thread them onto yarn as for beads. To work sequin, bring yarn to front of work.

**2** Slide sequin close to work and, with sequin still in front, move yarn to back of work, then continue to work as usual. Work all sequins in this manner, adding sequins to right side of work.

**3** If you are working in garter stitch, add sequins on wrong side rows, sliding sequin close to work; then continue to knit until ready to add next sequin.

**4** On following row (right side of work), knit all the stitches: The sequins will naturally remain visible from this side. Complete decoration, adding sequins every other row at desired positions.

# jacquard stitch

This method of knitting allows you to make garments enhanced with multicolored designs in strikingly bright or subtly subdued hues.

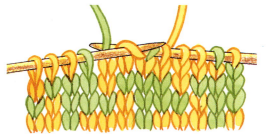

## ■ work in panels

**1** When you work a piece with colors knitted in vertical panels or stripes, use a separate ball of yarn for each section, even if the color is repeated across the row. To avoid holes in work when you change colors, twist yarns on back of work by dropping color just completed and bringing new color under old and up to continue working. Be sure to twist the yarns every row, keeping both yarns on the wrong side of your work.

**2** On wrong side rows, twist yarns as before and keep yarn on this side to purl stitches. This way, all yarn twists remain on wrong side of work.

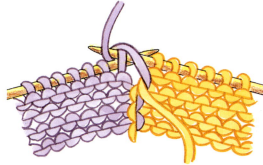

## ■ jacquard in two colors

**1** If you need to alternate colors often (every 3 or 4 stitches) in same row, carry both colors across wrong side of work. On knit rows, hold yarn not being used in back and to left, to make it easier to use other color. You can hold 1 color in your right hand as usual, and the other in your left hand as for continental knitting (see page 16), alternating methods to work each color as needed.

**2** On wrong side rows, follow same procedure, always keeping yarns on wrong side. Throughout, be careful to maintain uniform tension so stitches are worked evenly without being too tight or loose.

### Working Colors with Bobbins

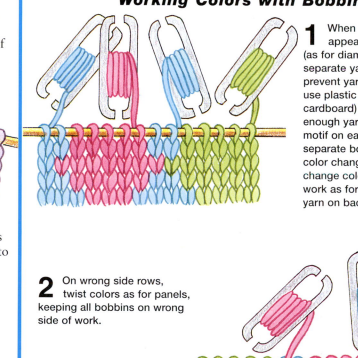

**1** When a number of colors appear in small motifs (as for diamonds, shown), use separate yarn for each. To prevent yarns from tangling, use plastic (or homemade cardboard) bobbins. Wrap enough yarn to work one motif on each bobbin, using a separate bobbin for each color change across row. To change colors on right side, work as for panels, twisting yarn on back.

**2** On wrong side rows, twist colors as for panels, keeping all bobbins on wrong side of work.

# jacquard stitch

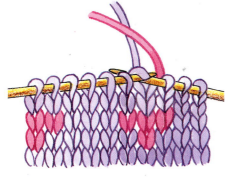

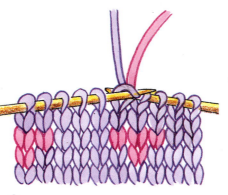

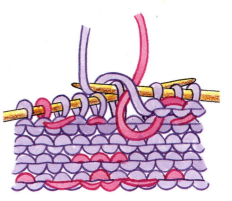

## ■ jacquard with woven yarns

**1** If motifs are more widely spaced, it is a good idea to catch loose (unworked) yarn into back of work. This prevents long strands which make it difficult to work and can be pulled out of place when garment is worn. To catch loose yarn, on right side rows, carry working yarn in your right hand as usual and unworked yarn over left index finger.

**2** Then insert right needle into next stitch and below the loose yarn, knit stitch (drawing through only working color), then knit next stitch as usual with needle above loose yarn (yarn is caught in back of work).

**3** On wrong side of work, catch loose yarn by inserting right needle into next stitch and under loose color and purl stitch.

**4** Then purl next stitch with yarn over loose yarn. Repeat working 2 stitches in this manner to catch yarn, always leaving yarn on wrong side of work.

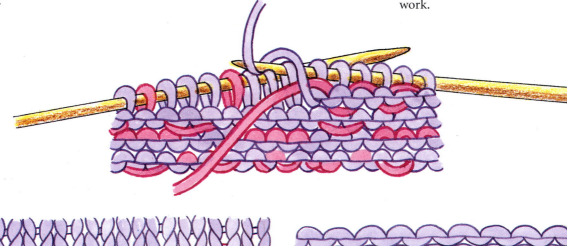

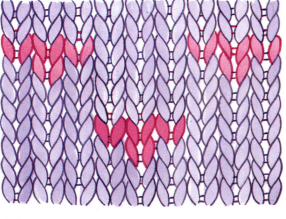

**5** This is how work will look on the right side.

**6** On wrong side, work will look like this if you catch loose yarn every other stitch. **NOTE:** Contrast yarn is not carried on single color rows on this pattern.

# smocking on knits

The smock stitch can be embroidered on knitted pieces as well as on fabric in a variety of patterns. There are also some knitted stitches that produce smocking without using embroidery.

## ▪ smock stitch on rib stitch

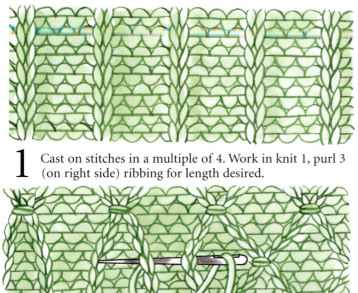

**1** Cast on stitches in a multiple of 4. Work in knit 1, purl 3 (on right side) ribbing for length desired.

**2** Use same yarn, or a contrasting color, to embroider smock stitch, stitching 2 backstitches at each rib joining.

**3** Join ribs in pairs, alternating pairs in following smocking row, to form diamond pattern.

## ▪ smock stitch on stockinette stitch

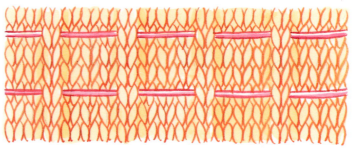

**1** Knit in stockinette stitch for desired length, and for a width about three times finished width. With contrasting color yarn, sew parallel lines across, picking up same vertical stitches on each sewn row. Evenly space vertical stitch rows and sewn lines, spacing them by thickness of yarn.

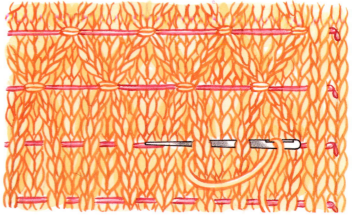

**2** With same color yarn, attach yarn and start at upper right corner. To smock, join vertical ribs together in pairs, securing each joining with 2 backstitches. In traditional smocking, 2 horizontal rows are worked together, working first in upper row then in lower one, alternating pairs of ribs (see illustration, left); this provides elasticity, which is important for fabric. In knitting, however, you can just work across, following parallel lines, and securing yarn at end of row. Starting at right edge again, work next parallel line and skip first rib, then join in pairs across, skip last rib. Alternate ribs to form diamonds.

**3** Complete smocking and remove colored yarn guidelines.

# smocking on knits

■ **knitted smocking pattern**

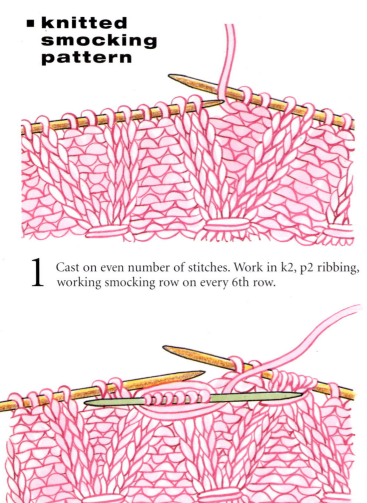

1 Cast on even number of stitches. Work in k2, p2 ribbing, working smocking row on every 6th row.

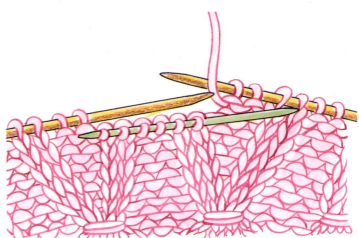

2 Smocking row: * Connect 2 ribs by placing 6 stitches (knit 2, purl 2, knit 2) on a double-pointed (dp) needle and hold in front of work.

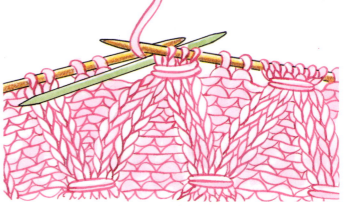

3 Bring yarn to front, wrap it around stitches on dp needle, wrapping it twice from left around front to right, and to back again.

4 Now work those same stitches from dp needle (knit 2, purl 2, knit 2).

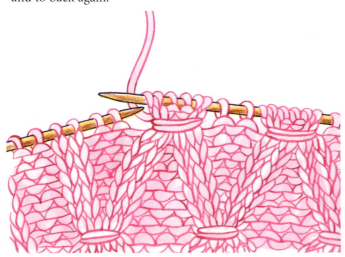

5 Purl the next 2 stitches. Starting with next 6 stitches on left needle, repeat from * across row.

6 Continue in ribbing and work smocking row every 6th row, alternating pairs of ribs, to form diamond pattern.

# knitting cables

**C**ables are one of the most interesting knitted patterns. They are made with a cable needle or a double-pointed needle that allows you to move the stitches you wish to intertwine.

Most cables are worked on the right side on a background of reversed stockinette stitch (purl side) to makes the cables stand out.

You can vary cables as you like, changing width (number of stitches used) and distance between twists (crossovers).

A classic cable is formed with an equal width and length between crossings, but this is not a hard and fast rule. There is a general rule that cables should be worked on an even number of stitches so you can divide the stitches in half.

A few cables are worked with fewer or more stitches on some rows than originally cast on; at some point, the number returns to the original within each repeated section.

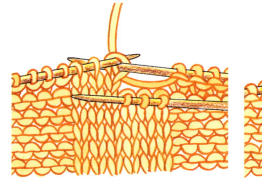 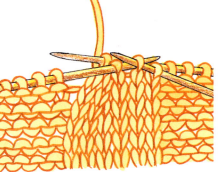

### ■ simple cable with left twist

**1** Work cable on 6 stitches as follows: Work in stockinette stitch for a few rows, ending with a purl row. * Cable twist row: Place 3 first stitches on double pointed (dp) needle and hold in front of work. Knit next 3 stitches on left needle.

**2** Return 3 stitches on dp needle to left needle and knit them.

**3** Continue as before until you reach next cable twist. Repeat from * to work cable.

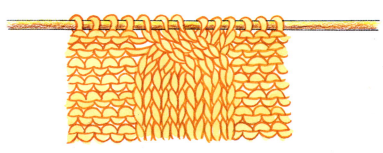

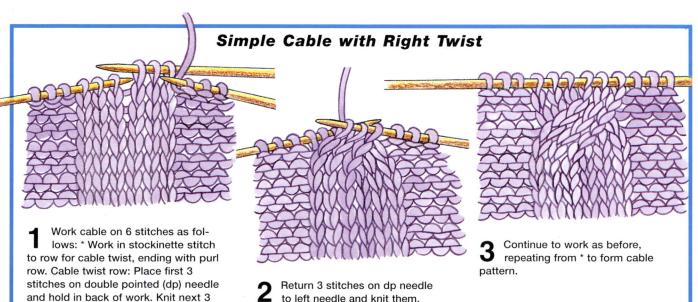

## Simple Cable with Right Twist

**1** Work cable on 6 stitches as follows: * Work in stockinette stitch to row for cable twist, ending with purl row. Cable twist row: Place first 3 stitches on double pointed (dp) needle and hold in back of work. Knit next 3 stitches on left needle.

**2** Return 3 stitches on dp needle to left needle and knit them.

**3** Continue to work as before, repeating from * to form cable pattern.

# knitting cables

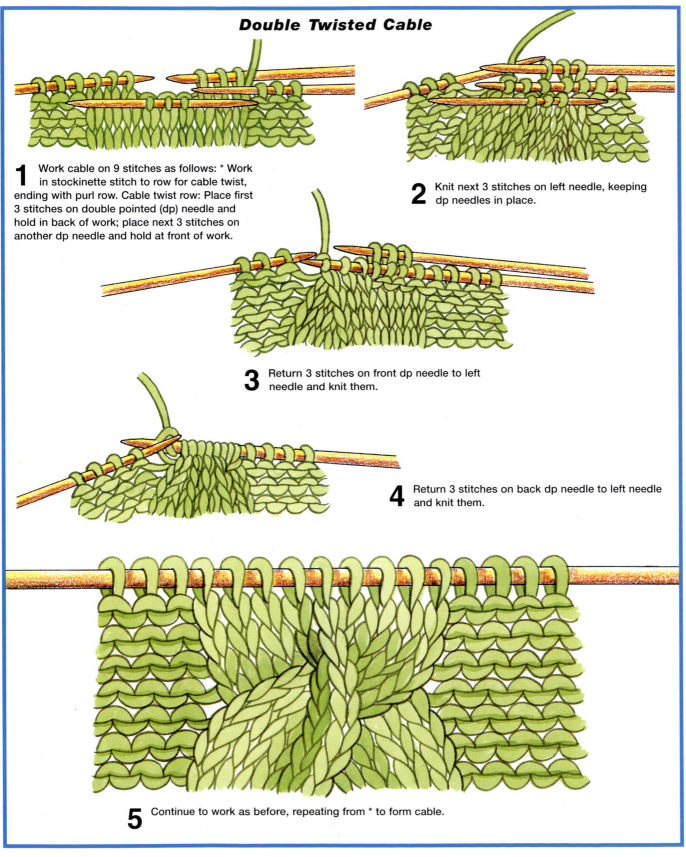

### Double Twisted Cable

**1** Work cable on 9 stitches as follows: * Work in stockinette stitch to row for cable twist, ending with purl row. Cable twist row: Place first 3 stitches on double pointed (dp) needle and hold in back of work; place next 3 stitches on another dp needle and hold at front of work.

**2** Knit next 3 stitches on left needle, keeping dp needles in place.

**3** Return 3 stitches on front dp needle to left needle and knit them.

**4** Return 3 stitches on back dp needle to left needle and knit them.

**5** Continue to work as before, repeating from * to form cable.

# bobbles

Small, large, or elongated, bobbles can add texture to your work. They are generally done with knitting needles, but there is also a version made with a crochet hook.

## ■ the bobble

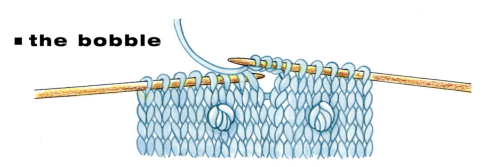

**1** On knit row, work in stockinette stitch to desired position for bobble. To make bobble: Increase in next stitch by working * knit 1 stitch, knit 1 twisted stitch; repeat from * once more (4 stitches worked in 1 stitch).

**2** Slipping 1 stitch over next without knitting it, bind off added stitches in order until you are left with only 1 stitch.

**3** On next (purl) row, purl bobble stitch as usual. Continue to work bobbles on right side of work, spacing them as you like.

## ■ the long bobble

**1** On knit row, work in stockinette stitch to desired position for bobble. To make long bobble: Insert needle through stitch 4 rows below next stitch, wrap yarn over needle tip and pull up a long loop, then work * yarn over, make another long loop stitch in same stitch as before; repeat from * 2 more times (7 stitches are worked in one).

**2** Transfer these 7 stitches to left needle and knit them together with next stitch as one.

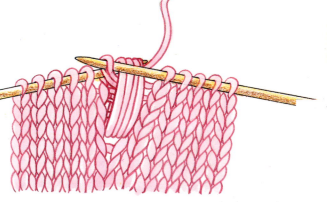

**3** On next (purl) row, purl bobble stitch as usual. Continue to work bobbles on right side of work, spacing them as you like.

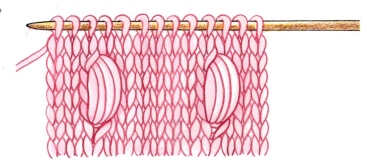

# bobbles

## ■ the big bobble

**1** Work to desired position for bobble. Increase in next stitch by working * knit 1 stitch, knit 1 twisted stitch; repeat from * once more (4 stitches worked in one stitch). Then * turn work, purl 4 stitches, turn again and knit 4; repeat from * once more.

**2** Slipping 1 stitch over next without knitting it, bind off added stitches in order until you are left with only 1 stitch.

**3** On next row, work the bobble stitch as usual. Continue to work bobbles on right side of work, spacing them as you like.

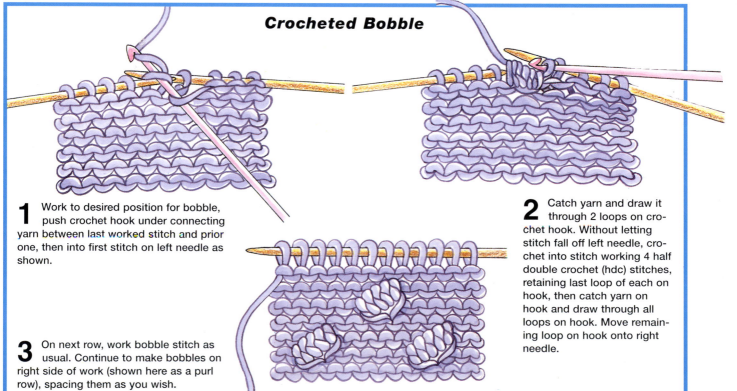

### Crocheted Bobble

**1** Work to desired position for bobble, push crochet hook under connecting yarn between last worked stitch and prior one, then into first stitch on left needle as shown.

**2** Catch yarn and draw it through 2 loops on crochet hook. Without letting stitch fall off left needle, crochet into stitch working 4 half double crochet (hdc) stitches, retaining last loop of each on hook, then catch yarn on hook and draw through all loops on hook. Move remaining loop on hook onto right needle.

**3** On next row, work bobble stitch as usual. Continue to make bobbles on right side of work (shown here as a purl row), spacing them as you wish.

# fur stitch

This is an easy technique for edges on jackets, afghans, pillows, and other accessories for the house. Rows are worked making looped fringes that are long or short.

## ■ a loop in every stitch

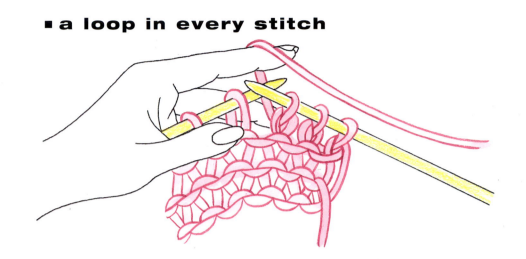

**1** Use thin yarns. Cast on desired number of stitches. Knit 5 rows in garter stitch. Work loops on next wrong side row as follows: Knit 1st stitch; wrap yarn under left index finger, then back over top of finger (as shown).

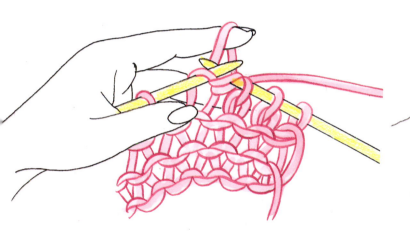

**2** * Catch back of finger loop on right needle, then knit next stitch drawing both loops (from finger loop and new stitch) through stitch as usual, but do not let it fall from needle.

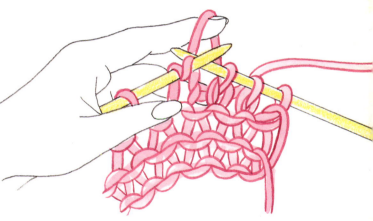

**3** Keeping finger loop still wrapped around your finger, slide both picked-up loop and new stitch (made in previous step) from right needle back onto left needle.

**4** Knit loop, new stitch, and original stitch together in a twisted knit, anchoring loop. Drop loop off finger and rewrap yarn around finger as before; repeat from * across row, knitting last stitch as usual. Work loops on every other row so they all fall on same side of work.

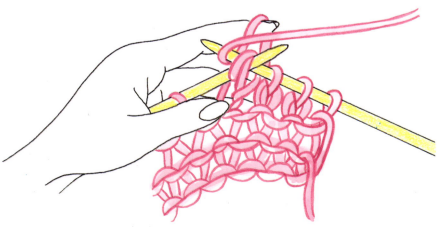

# fur stitch

## ■ longer and thinner loops

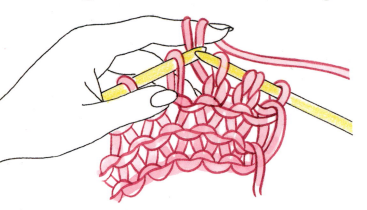 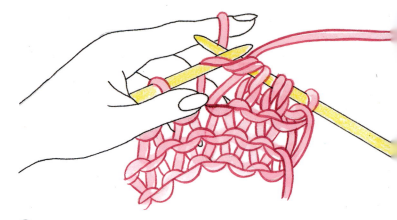

**1** Knit 2 rows in garter stitch. Work loops on next row as follows: Knit 1 for edge, then to work first loop, * wrap yarn around left index finger as shown.

**2** Insert right needle in next stitch and, without knitting it, draw 2 loops of yarn wrapped around finger through same stitch. Slide old stitch off needle.

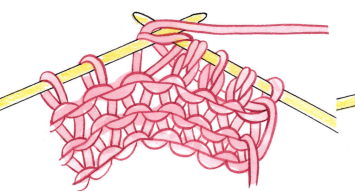

**3** Keeping remaining loop on finger extended, knit next stitch and let finger loop fall. Repeat from * across row, ending with knit stitch at edge.

**4** On next row, knit all stitches and over each loop, knit the 2 loops together in a knit twist. Knit 2 more rows in garter stitch.

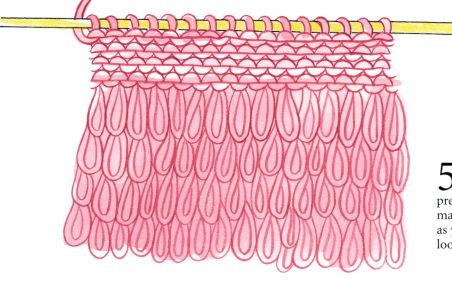

**5** Repeat these 6 rows for pattern as shown. If you prefer, work 2 fewer or as many more garter stitch rows as you like, always forming loops on same side of work.

# fringes and pompons

These decorations help add a touch of elegance or fun to all sorts of things from hats, shawls, and afghans to baby clothes.

## ■ pompon

**1** Cut out 2 same-sized cardboard circles, the diameter a bit larger than desired size of pompon, to allow for center hole and final trimming.

Cut out a hole at center (the bigger the hole, the fuller the pompon will be) and slit at one side so you can easily extract pompon.

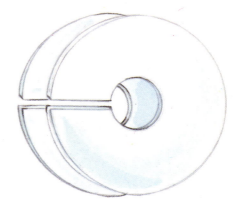

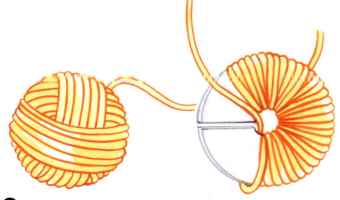

**2** Hold discs together and wrap yarn around them. Thread yarn needle with yarn, if you like, to make wrapping easier.

Pompon fullness depends on amount of yarn wrapped.

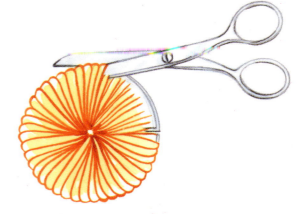

**3** Insert the tip of a pair of scissors in between cardboard discs and cut all strands around outer edge.

**4** Gently pull discs apart and wrap a length of matching yarn several times around center of cut strands.
Tie yarn very tightly with a strong knot.
Leave yarn ends of tie to attach pompon.

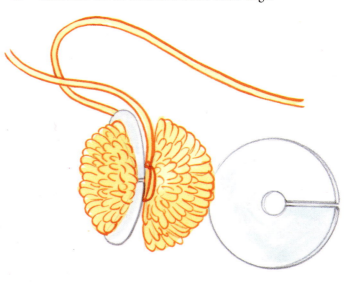

**5** Remove 2 (reusable) discs from pompons. Then fluff up pompon with your hand. Use scissors to trim any long strands to make an evenly rounded pompon.

# fringes and pompons

## ■ fringe in one knot

**1** Cut strip of cardboard to desired length of fringe. Wrap yarn around cardboard without stretching it.

   With scissors, cut yarn along one end of cardboard to make strands of an even length.

   Separate into groups of 2 to 8 strands, depending on thickness of yarn.

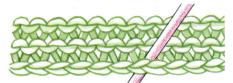

**2** Working along wrong side of edge to be fringed, insert crochet hook into edge as shown. Fold enough yarn strands for 1 fringe in half. Holding folded center up, catch loops on hook.

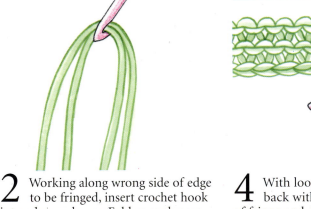

**3** Draw loops through edge with hook.

## Fringe with Double Knot

**1** Make long fringes and attach to edge, as indicated, at left. Then, leaving half of first fringe free, knot together half of each fringe with half of the next.

**2** Before tightening these knots, adjust height with a pin, prodding them higher or lower to make row of knots even. Trim ends evenly.

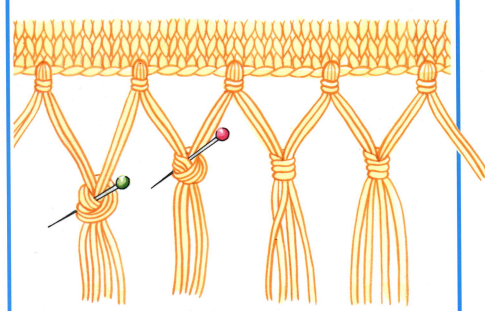

**4** With loops still on hook, reach back with hook to catch yarn ends of fringe and draw them through loops.

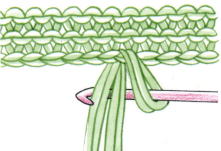

**5** Pull ends to tighten knot.
   Knot fringes in this manner, spacing them as you like. In general, space thin fringes closer together than thicker one to make a nice full edge. Trim ends even.

# baby booties

**1** Begin working from ankle. Cast on needed stitches and * work in stockinette stitch for about 1¼ inches (3 cm), ending with knit row. Work eyelet row (k2tog, yarn over), purl next row; repeat from * once more.

**2** Continue in stockinette stitch for ¾ inch (2 cm) more (cuff). Divide stitches in 3 parts, placing each side section on a holder.

**3** Continue on center stitches only for about 2¾ inches (7 cm); then decrease 1 stitch on each side every other row twice (top of foot).

**4** Use crochet hook to pick up stitches on both sides of foot, adding stitches from holders at each end.

**5** Continue on all stitches for about ¾ inches/2 cm (sides of foot).

# baby booties

**7** Now continue on sole, but now at each end of row, decrease by knitting together end heel stitch with adjoining side stitch. Continue in this manner until you complete sole, ending at the heel.

**6** Keep all stitches on needle, marking center stitches. Now work only on center stitches to work sole, increasing 1 stitch on each side every row twice. Move markers to include increases (toe).

**8** Use a yarn needle to work weaving stitch (see page 71) to connect stitches of one side to corresponding half of sole stitches; then connect those on other side in same manner.

**9** Seam center edges of cuffs.
Fold under top cuff edge at first eyelet row; sew in place. Thread a cord (see page 48) through second eyelet row.

# mittens 1

**1** Cast on stitches needed for wrist edge. Work in k1, p1 ribbing for desired length. Now work in stockinette stitch and begin thumb shaping. Mark center stitch with colored yarn. On knit row, increase 2 stitches in stitch just before and just after marked center one; increase at outer edges of thumb shaping in this manner every 4 rows. Work until there are enough stitches for width of thumb. Cast on 2 stitches at each end of thumb section.

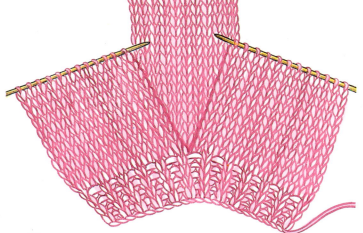

**2** Continue working only on thumb stitches, placing other stitches on another needle or holder.

**4** Work to desired length of hand. Mark center to divide work. Shape tip on knit rows by working 2 edge stitches at the ends of each section; work 1 decrease just within each edge (4 stitches decreased on row). Repeat decreases every other row 2 or 3 times, then bind off remaining stitches.

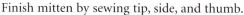

**5** Finish mitten by sewing tip, side, and thumb.

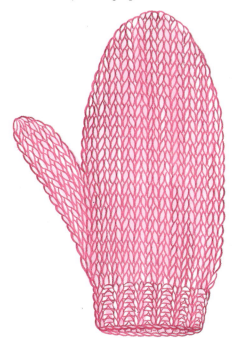

**3** When thumb is desired length, ending with purl row, shape tip by knitting 2 stitches together across next row; purl 1 row; knit 2 stitches together across row. Cut yarn and thread in yarn needle; sew remaining stitches and draw them together; secure. Now work first section of hand stitches, pick up 2 stitches on each side at base of thumb, work other hand section.

115

# mittens 2

**1** Cast on for wrist edge. Work k1, p1 for ribbing. Work mitten in stockinette stitch, starting thumb shaping on first knit row by increasing 1 stitch in first stitch (2 thumb stitches). Continue, shaping thumb by increasing 1 stitch at beginning and end of thumb section every knit row, until thumb is needed width. Place thumb stitches on extra needle or holder. Then continue working on hand stitches up to shaped finger area. Divide hand into 2 sections; place one section on holder. Continue on other side, decreasing 1 stitch at each edge every 4 rows up to top. Bind off remaining stitches.

**2** Work other hand section the same way.

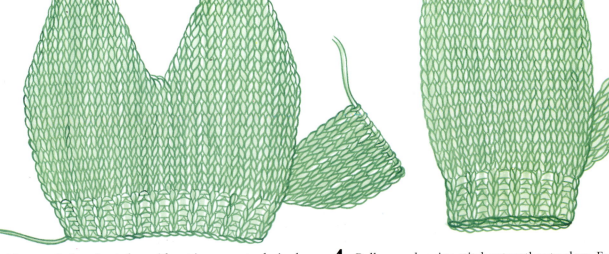

**3** Now work thumb stitches without increases to desired length. Cut yarn; thread end through thumb stitches as shown.

**4** Pull yarn, drawing stitches together to close. Fold mitten and thumb in half. Starting and ending at wrist edge, seam outer edges of hand and thumb; then sew unsewn slanted edge of thumb to opening on other hand section.

# gloves

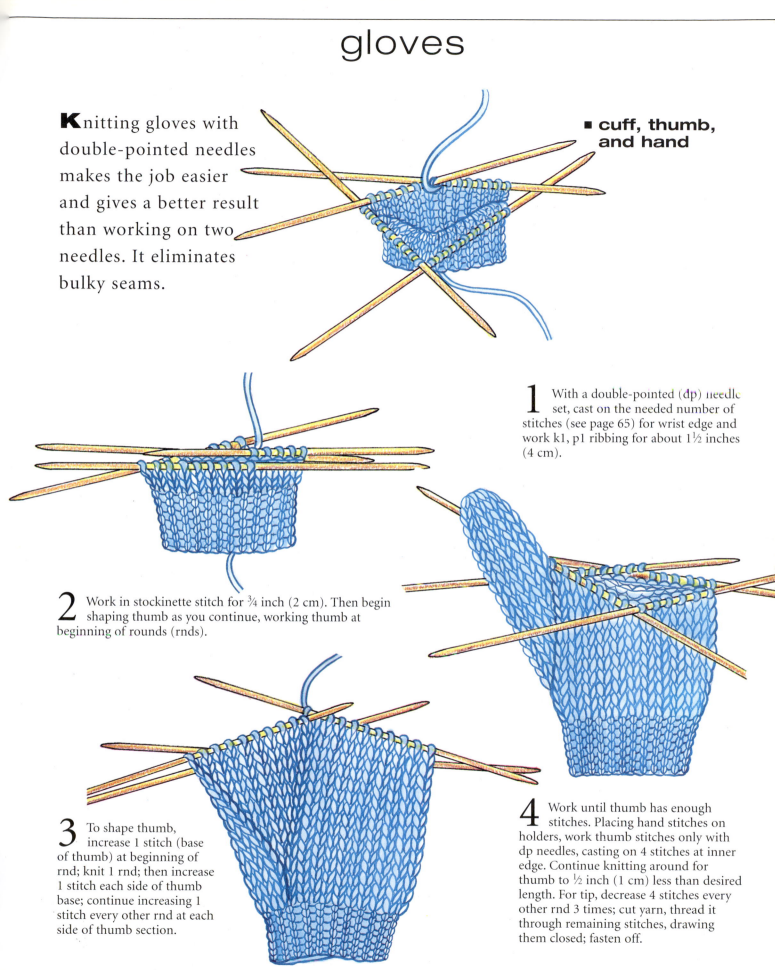

Knitting gloves with double-pointed needles makes the job easier and gives a better result than working on two needles. It eliminates bulky seams.

■ **cuff, thumb, and hand**

**1** With a double-pointed (dp) needle set, cast on the needed number of stitches (see page 65) for wrist edge and work k1, p1 ribbing for about 1½ inches (4 cm).

**2** Work in stockinette stitch for ¾ inch (2 cm). Then begin shaping thumb as you continue, working thumb at beginning of rounds (rnds).

**3** To shape thumb, increase 1 stitch (base of thumb) at beginning of rnd; knit 1 rnd; then increase 1 stitch each side of thumb base; continue increasing 1 stitch every other rnd at each side of thumb section.

**4** Work until thumb has enough stitches. Placing hand stitches on holders, work thumb stitches only with dp needles, casting on 4 stitches at inner edge. Continue knitting around for thumb to ½ inch (1 cm) less than desired length. For tip, decrease 4 stitches every other rnd 3 times; cut yarn, thread it through remaining stitches, drawing them closed; fasten off.

117

# gloves

**■ making the fingers**

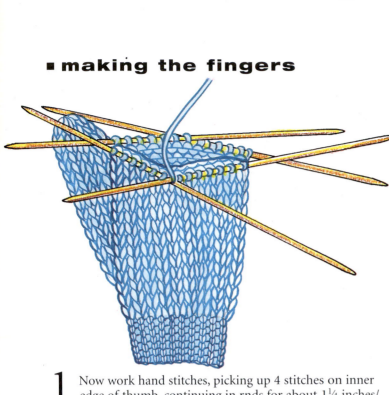

**1** Now work hand stitches, picking up 4 stitches on inner edge of thumb, continuing in rnds for about 1¼ inches/ 3 cm (or desired length to start fingers). Count stitches on needles; divide number as equally as possible for 4 fingers.

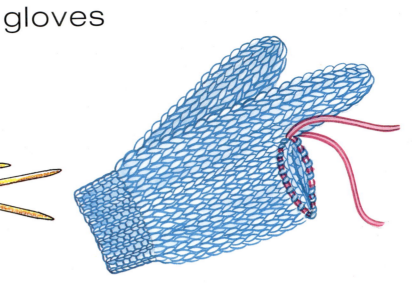

**2** Work index finger, using equal number from back and palm, to make up needed number, then cast on 3 stitches for bridge to middle finger. Place remaining stitches on yarn-strand holder. Work in rnds on dp needles as for thumb to desired length. Shape tip by decreasing 4 stitches every other rnd twice. Close tip as for thumb.

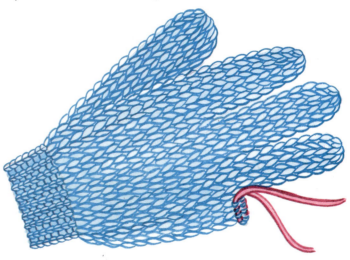

**4** Work ring finger same as for middle finger, picking up 3 stitches from bridge and casting on 3 stitches for next bridge to little finger.

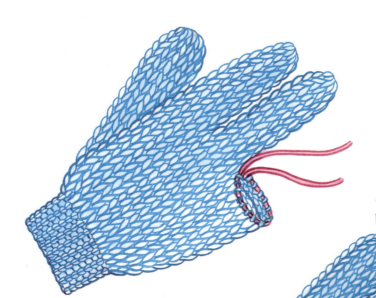

**3** Place middle finger stitches (from palm and back of hand) on needles, picking up 3 stitches from previous bridge and casting on 3 stitches as bridge to ring finger. Work as for index finger.

**5** Finally, work little finger stitches, picking up 3 stitches from previous bridge, and work as for index finger, but making it a bit shorter.

# aran isle sweater 1

**■ turtleneck, shoulders, and start of front**

**A** traditional Aran Isle sweater is knitted in one unit with double-pointed needles or a circular needle, and requires no sewing. Each section is knitted by setting aside and picking up the stitches in a set order, and using a lavish variety of cables, zigzags, lattice, or diamonds typical of the little island of Aran.

**1** With double-pointed (dp) needles, or small circular needle, cast on stitches as needed to work turtleneck. Work a few rows in tubular knit, then continue working around in k1, p1 ribbing.

**2** When turtleneck is about 5 inches (12 cm) long, if you are not already using dp needles, divide stitches into 4 equal parts and place them on separate holders.

**3** Continue on one side only and work simple cables for a length equal to width of one shoulder; place these stitches on holder and work other shoulder, on opposite side of turtleneck, to correspond to first shoulder.

# aran isle sweater 1

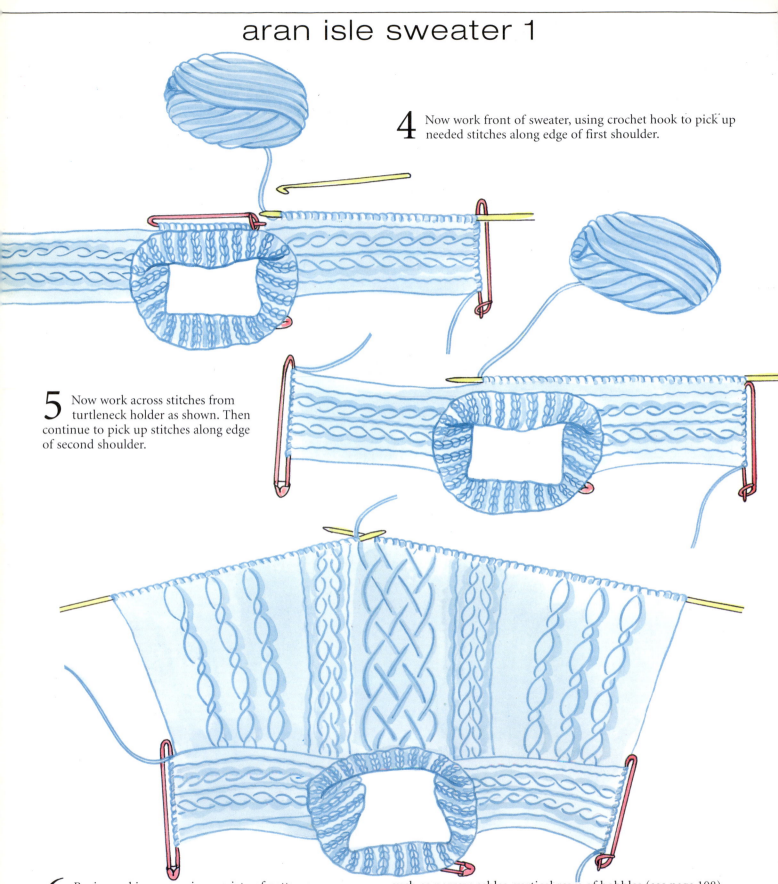

**4** Now work front of sweater, using crochet hook to pick up needed stitches along edge of first shoulder.

**5** Now work across stitches from turtleneck holder as shown. Then continue to pick up stitches along edge of second shoulder.

**6** Begin working across in a variety of patterns. Traditionally, the center panel is the same width as the turtleneck and is worked with lattice, diamonds, or a wide cable pattern on a reverse stockinette stitch background. Remaining stitches at sides are worked with smaller patterns, such as narrow cables, vertical rows of bobbles (see page 108), and moss stitches. Check your gauge on selected patterns to calculate number of stitches needed. The variety of suitable patterns and their placement means you can make a sweater that is both traditional and individual.

# aran isle sweater 2

## ■ neck opening and completing the front and back

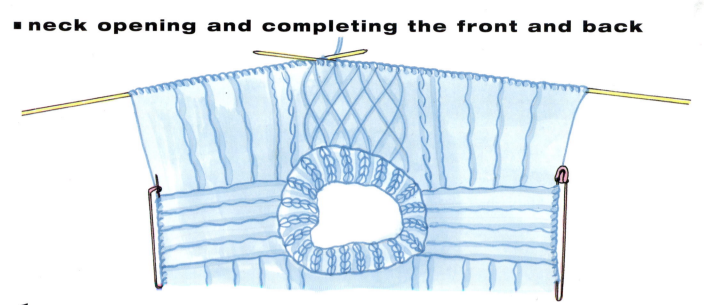

**1** Work on all stitches of front down to start of armholes, about 7 inches (18 cm) below shoulder section. Place front stitches on a holder. Then pick up stitches for back along opposite edge of shoulder and turtleneck section, and work back exactly the same as front to start of armholes.

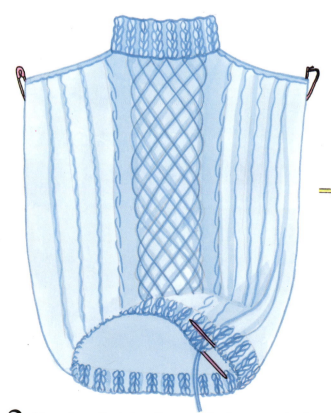

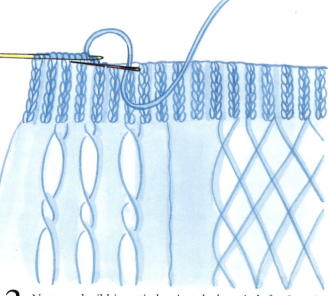

**2** Now place all stitches, front and back, onto a circular needle. Casting on about 6 stitches at each armhole edge, knit around in rounds (rnds). Because you will now be working in rnds on right side only (not rows as before), you need to adapt patterns accordingly to keep them as established. Continue working down to within 2¼ inches (6 cm) of desired finished length. Now discontinue patterns and work in k1, p1 ribbing for 2¼ inches (6 cm).

**3** Now work ribbing stitches in tubular stitch for 2 or 4 rows; use yarn needle to close stitches with weaving stitch. Front and back are now completed.

# aran isle sweater 2

## ■ sleeves and finishing your work

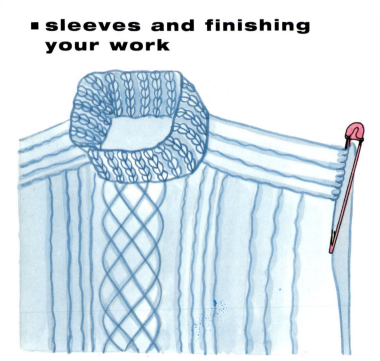

**1** Now place stitches of one shoulder onto needle. Use crochet hook to pick up stitches around armhole, distributing them onto dp needles or a short circular needle.

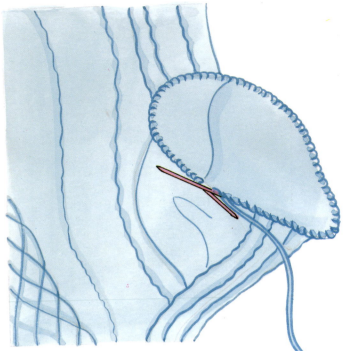

**2** Work on all stitches as follows: On center part of sleeve, continue motif of shoulder and work remaining side stitches in moss stitch or one of the pattern stitches used for sides of front panel.

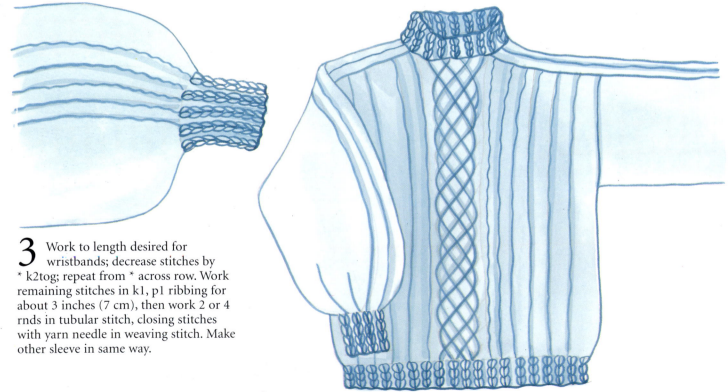

**3** Work to length desired for wristbands; decrease stitches by * k2tog; repeat from * across row. Work remaining stitches in k1, p1 ribbing for about 3 inches (7 cm), then work 2 or 4 rnds in tubular stitch, closing stitches with yarn needle in weaving stitch. Make other sleeve in same way.

**4** The sweater is now completed and, following Irish tradition, it has been made in only one piece without any sewing.

# socks

The classic sock is knitted around starting from the top edge. The ankle can be worked with any pattern or colored design you like, but in this example the sock is worked with two simple cables on a background of purls.

## ■ edge, ankle, and heel

**1** With double pointed (dp) needles, cast on needed stitches for top (ankle) edge (see page 65); work in rounds (rnds) in k1, p1 ribbing for about an inch (2½ cm).

**2** Now work in desired pattern until piece is 12 inches (30 cm) from beginning (for a short sock).

**3** To shape heel, divide stitches in 2 equal parts (top of foot and sole). Work only on the sole, knitting back and forth on 2 needles for 2½ inches (6¼ cm). Adjust pattern to work in rows to keep continuity of pattern. Now turn heel as follows.

**4** Divide stitches in 3 parts, leaving more stitches in center (for example, if there are 30 stitches, keep 8 stitches on sides and 14 stitches at center). Work short rows on center stitches, decreasing 1 side stitch at end of each row as follows: On knit rows, knit to last center stitch and slip this stitch, knit next side stitch and pass slipped stitch over it; on purl rows, purl last center stitch and first side stitch together as one. Work until all side stitches are decreased.

# socks

## ■ the gusset, sole, and toe

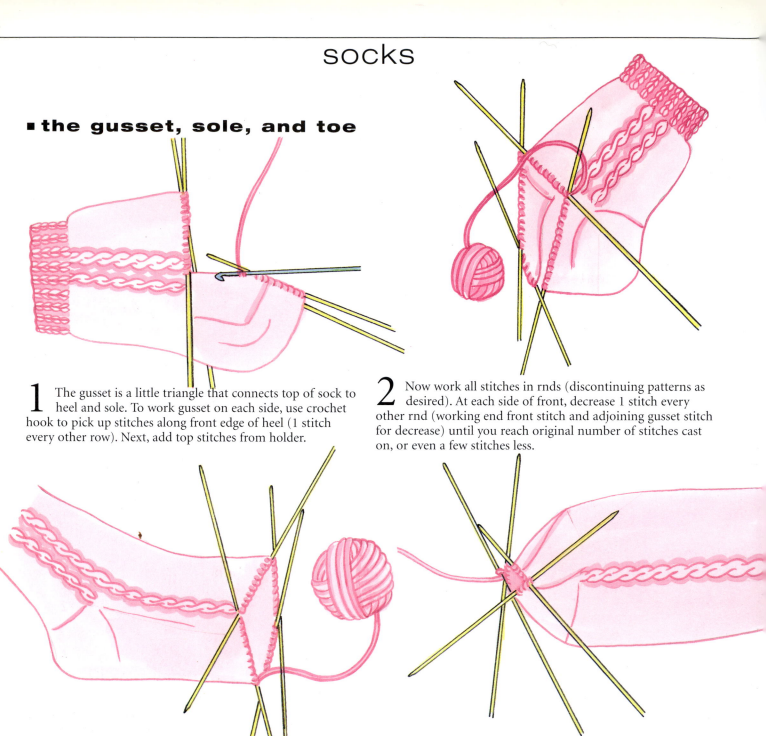

**1** The gusset is a little triangle that connects top of sock to heel and sole. To work gusset on each side, use crochet hook to pick up stitches along front edge of heel (1 stitch every other row). Next, add top stitches from holder.

**2** Now work all stitches in rnds (discontinuing patterns as desired). At each side of front, decrease 1 stitch every other rnd (working end front stitch and adjoining gusset stitch for decrease) until you reach original number of stitches cast on, or even a few stitches less.

**3** Now continue to work in rnds to complete foot, about 2 inches (5 cm) less than finished length.

**4** Shape toe by decreasing 1 stitch at each side of foot and at center of top and sole (4 evenly spaced decreases on rnd); work decreases every other rnd.

**5** When you have only a few stitches left, cut yarn and thread yarn end in yarn needle. Pass it through stitches and draw them tightly; fasten off.

# quilted knits

Finishing a knitted garment with quilting adds a decorative touch and warmth by joining several layers to the original knitted piece. Quilting is good for jackets, coats, and other outdoor garments.

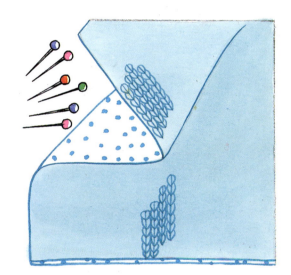

**1** Block knitted pieces. Lay each piece on the lining fabric, right sides together. Pin layers together around edges. Following edge of pieces, cut out fabric adding a ½-inch (1-cm) seam allowance all around.

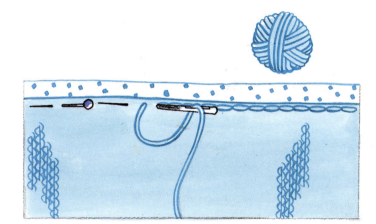

**2** Using matching yarn (if thin enough) or thread, sew knitted edges of each piece to the lining with backstitch, as shown. Leave edges to be joined to other pieces open; be sure to have at least one opening on each piece for turning.

**3** Turn work right-side out. Gently press edges with iron to flatten them; adjust any minor ripples between layers by carefully blocking knit section again.

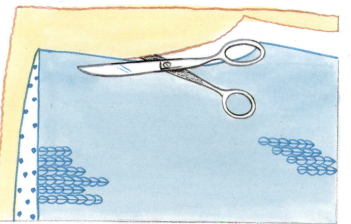

**4** Cut inner layer from quilt batting as follows: Place knitted parts on top of batting and cut batting carefully following edges.

# quilted knits

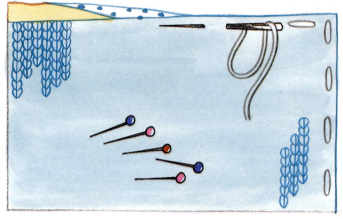

**5** Insert batting between the 2 layers, making it fit outline of piece.

**6** Pin around edges, leaving lining seam allowance extended for joining edges, and, at edges not to be joined, folding lining under knit at open edge (as shown) and pinning through all 3 layers. Baste all around edge.

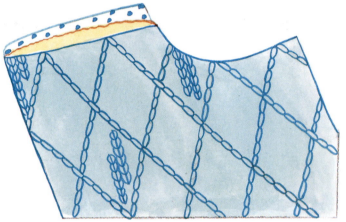

**7** Lay piece on flat surface. Use a line of pins to mark off parallel diagonal lines to form a diamond pattern (as shown), spacing lines about 2 inches (5 cm) apart. Sew along lines to quilt piece.

**8** Complete quilting each piece to edge. If desired, reinforce quilting by machine, stitching very carefully with same color thread, or, better, hand-embroider lines in a matching or contrasting color.

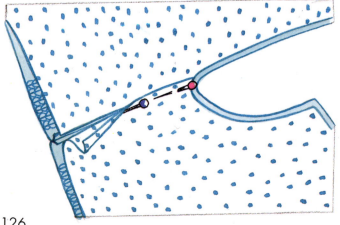

**9** Seam knitted edges as usual (at shoulders, underarm, and so on). Finish inside by folding under seam allowances of lining as shown and sew seam closed.

# knitted patchwork

The finished work made with this technique looks like traditional patchwork, but it is knitted in one unit without piecing. Use the technique to make garments, afghans, and pillows.

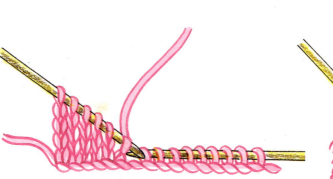

## ■ base triangle

**1** The example shown is worked on a multiple of 6 stitches. With color A yarn, cast on desired number of stitches and work as follows: P1, turn work around; k1, turn work, p1, then p next stitch from starting row, turn work; continue in stockinette stitch until you have used the first 6 stitches.

**2** Put these 6 stitches on a holder and work across row, making a triangle on each group of 6 stitches, until you have used all stitches.

## ■ triangle at right edge and first square

**1** Second row of motifs begins with triangle as follows: Attach color B, then increase (inc) by knitting into base of first stitch (on color A triangle), then k this first A stitch from holder and pass inc stitch over it (1 B stitch remaining); turn work, p1 and inc in same stitch; turn, k1, slip 1, k next A stitch, pass slip stitch over it (psso), joining edges; turn, p across and inc 1 at edge; turn; k to last stitch, slip it, k1 A, and psso (joining); turn; continue in this manner, working inc at outer (right) edge and joining inner edge to A triangle.

**2** Place resulting 6 B stitches on holder and work first square as follows: With another needle, pick up 6 stitches along edge of first base triangle.

**3** Knit these stitches in stockinette stitch and join to next triangle at left edge as before, until all triangle stitches are worked (6 B stitches remain). Place on holder.

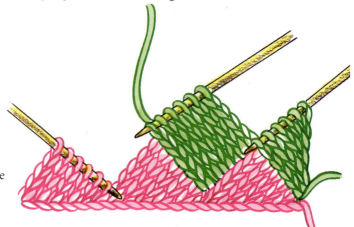

# knitted patchwork

## ■ triangle at left edge and finishing

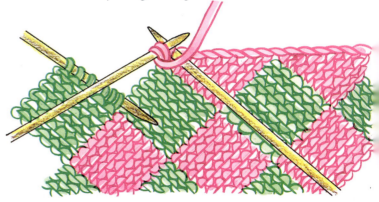

**1** Work across, making squares and joining each base triangle. Complete row with a triangle, picking up 6 stitches along edge of last base triangle. Turn; p2tog, p4, turn; k5, turn; p2tog, p3, turn; and continue in this manner, making a dec at outer (left) edge until there is 1 stitch left.

**2** Work next row of color A squares, from wrong (purl) side as follows: Pick up stitches by inserting needle from back of piece (right side of work). Pick up 5 stitches along edge of the end triangle, turn; k6, turn; p5, p2tog worked on last stitch of A square and stitch from next B square (joining); turn. Continue until joining is completed.

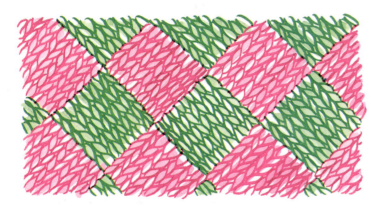

**3** Work across, making squares and joining to each B square. Turn. With B, working triangles at each end, work across making squares. Continue in this manner, alternating colors and alternating rows with end triangles and rows of squares only.

**4** When piece is the desired length, finish by filling in spaces across top as follows: Work as for the triangle at right edge, omitting increases and joining to first square. Then work center triangles, picking up 6 stitches, and work, decreasing at outer edge and joining to next square.

**5** Work across to last corner. Pick up 6 stitches and work, making 1 dec at each edge until all stitches are decreased. Fasten off.

# embroidery 1

Even a simple garment can be brought to life by some embroidery worked with a yarn needle. You can make any number of designs with this duplicate stitch.

### ■ duplicate stitch

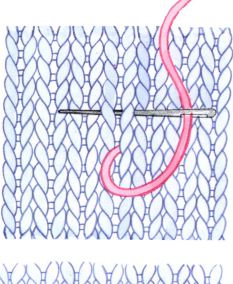

**1** Duplicate stitch is worked right to left on a stitch as follows: Thread yarn needle with colored yarn; anchor thread on back. Bring the needle up at base of stitch to be embroidered. Pass needle right under 2 threads of stitch above (as shown). Be careful not to snag strands.

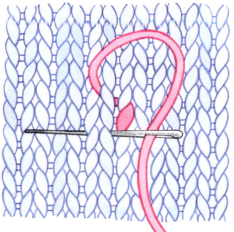

**2** Pull yarn through, neither too tightly or loosely, and exit at base of stitch being worked; bring needle up at base of next stitch to be worked on row.

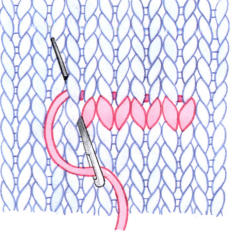

**3** Repeat this procedure for all stitches to be worked on row, exiting at base of last stitch. Bring needle up in base of first stitch (from left) to be worked on row above.

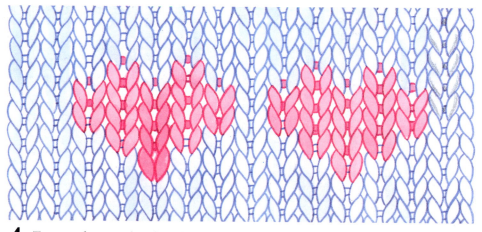

**4** Turn work around and work right to left as before, embroidering desired stitches on row. Continue in this manner until you complete design, always turning work for each row.

Work embroidery, following a charted design, on which each square represents 1 stitch and indicates color for that stitch.

# embroidery 1

### *Outline Stitch*

**To enhance duplicate stitches, complete motif with embroidered outline stitch.**

**1** Anchor yarn on wrong side with a few stitches. Bring needle to front of work along edge of motif and make a small stitch along outline, working around outline to the right. Bring needle to front again, near middle of stitch just made and very close to it on the left side. Make another stitch and bring it out at middle of previous stitch.

**2** Work around outline making tiny stitches at curves.

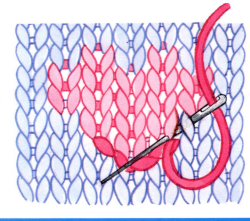
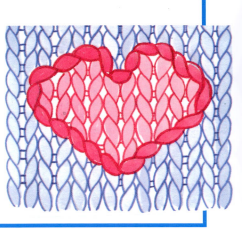

## ■ cross stitch

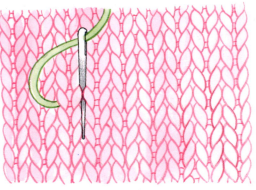

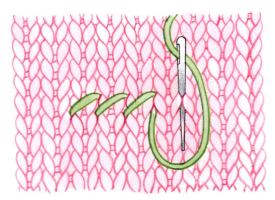

**1** Cross stitch can be embroidered in rows, or stitch by stitch. In sample shown, each cross stitch is worked over 1 knit stitch with a slanted stitch made across stitch. To work next adjoining stitch, bring needle straight down, under connecting yarn between stitches.

**2** Continue making slanted stitches in a row for desired number of stitches, with all slants worked in 1 direction.

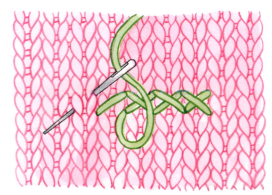

**3** Now work in opposite direction with stitches slanted other way; insert needle in same places as before to keep cross stitches square and even. You can also work in vertical rows. Always keep top thread of all stitches on any one embroidered piece slanting in same direction.

**4** Cross stitch can also be done stitch by stitch. After you make first slant on stitch, complete cross, making other slant before going on.

130

# embroidery 2

## ■ how to embroider with special needlework canvas

**1** Draw desired embroidery motif on paper. Use transfer paper (dressmaker's carbon) to trace design onto a piece of needlework canvas (special fabric with non-interlocked meshes, allowing fibers to be removed).

Pin fabric with design to knitted piece and baste it in place.

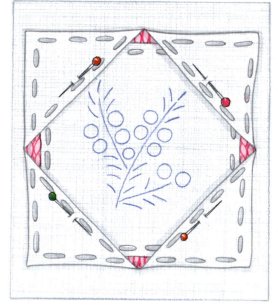

**2** Cut a piece of muslin bigger than embroidery hoops; cut center opening to expose design. Place muslin on knitted unit, with opening over design; baste it in place around opening.

### Embroidery onto Cardboard

Instead of needlework canvas, you can use tracing or tissue paper for your design. It is easier and eliminates using embroidery hoops.

This method works well for simple designs that allow paper to be torn away and removed easily.

**3** Place unit in embroidery hoops and adjust tension to keep taut but without pulling or stretching the knitting.

131

# embroidery 2

**4** Embroider design as desired, working through both fabric and knit layers.

**5** Remove embroidery hoops, then remove basting stitches and lift off muslin. Carefully trim away excess needlework canvas around design.

**6** Use tweezers to undo the fibers of needlework canvas.

**7** This is how the completed embroidery looks.

# embroidery 3

### ■ bullion stitch

**1** Bullion stitch, simple and decorative, is quite suitable for feminine garments. It can enhance plain stockinette stitch pieces as well as those with multicolored designs.
   Bring needle up at the spot you want to begin stitch. Then insert needle a short distance away (where stitch will end) and bring tip up in same place as before. Before drawing needle through, wrap yarn around tip a few times.

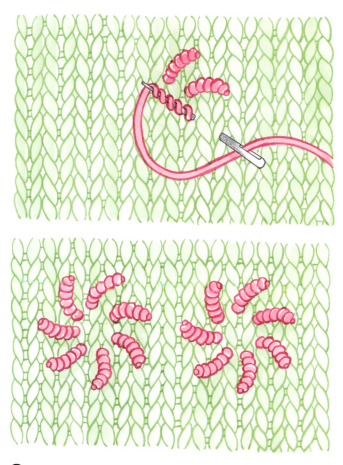

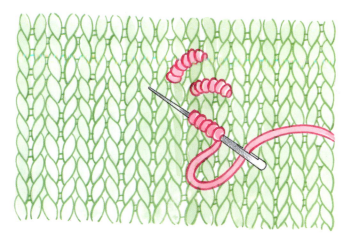

**2** Holding wraps firmly in place with left thumb and index finger, draw needle and yarn through the wraps.
   Drawing stitch backward to lie flat on work, insert needle once again at end of stitch to complete it. Bring needle tip out at spot for new stitch (actually to lower left of where it is shown in illustration).

**3** Work bullion stitches in this manner in a circle to form a flower as shown, or place as desired on work.

## French Knots

French knots, like bullion stitches, are wrapped-around stitches, but they are much smaller. They are often used for flower centers. Bring needle up where you want to work knot and wrap yarn around tip 2 or 3 times.
   Holding wraps in place, draw needle and yarn through the wraps, gently pulling yarn to tighten knot. Then insert yarn into work a tiny distance (1 yarn) from knot to anchor it on right side of work; bring needle up for next knot.

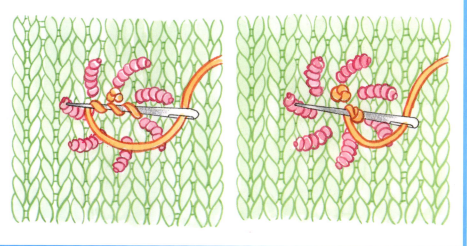

## ▪ padded satin stitch

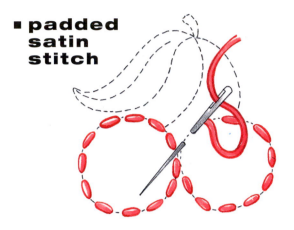

**1** Padded satin stitch is a solid stitch with a raised smooth surface. It can be worked using special needlework canvas (see page 131).
Sew around outline of stitch as shown.

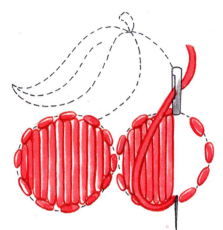

**2** Starting from left side, fill in outline, making long vertical stitches worked from bottom to top (as shown) and spaced closely together. (Long stitches are also formed on wrong side). Fill in outline, but stay within edges and maintain an even tension to keep work from puckering.

**3** When vertical stitches are completed, repeat operation to make horizontal stitches, covering previous stitches and keeping within outline.

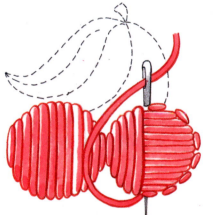

**4** With padding completed, finish stitch by working long, closely spaced vertical stitches, starting at left and covering padding and outline.

### Straight Stitch

Work with needlework canvas (see page 131). Use stitch to enhance edges of leaves and petals. Work (like satin stitch) from left to right by inserting needle downward from outline to inner part of motif; make small stitches and follow curves of design, closely spacing stitches. You can also use this stitch to follow a multicolored knitted design, embroidering directly onto knit stitches.

# embroidery 4

## ■ lazy daisy stitch

Simple to do, this stitch is widely used for making stylized flower petals and leaves. You can use tracing paper or needlework canvas (see page 131) to work designs.

The sample shows work moving in counterclockwise direction; you can work in other direction as well.

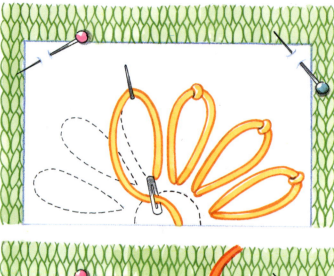

**1** Anchor yarn on wrong side and bring needle up at base of petal. Form a loop, holding it with left thumb and exit at same base, bringing needle up again just below tip of petal. Draw yarn through, making petal loop.

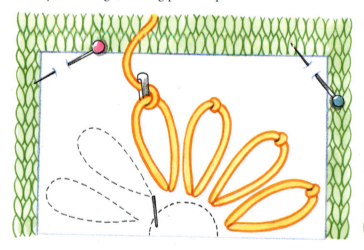

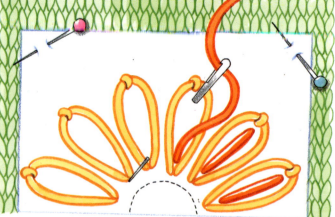

**2** Make tiny stitch over loop, anchoring it, and bring needle out at base of next petal.

**3** If desired, finish each lazy daisy stitch with a different color, working a long stitch at center of each petal.

### Chain Stitch

**With Needle:** Working downward, bring needle to right side and make a small loop for first stitch. Hold loop down with left thumb, then insert needle at base of loop and bring it out again at top of loop, catching it to form stitch (as shown). Repeat to work chain.

**With Crochet Hook:** Work straight up or on a slant, always moving upward. Use left hand to guide working yarn at the back. At start of chain, insert hook into knitted stitch and draw up loop. Then for first stitch, insert hook again above first insertion, catching working yarn at back and draw yarn through (as shown). Draw it through loop on hook, making a chain stitch. Repeat to make chain.

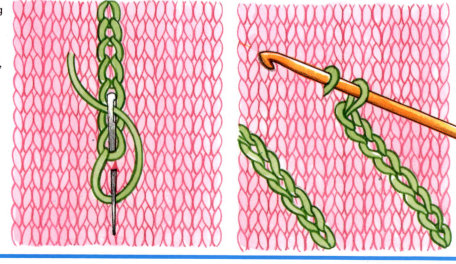

## ▪ long and short stitch

This is a useful stitch for filling complex areas and shading colors from dark to light. Use needlework canvas as shown (see page 131) unless design is very simple.

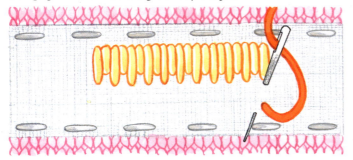

**1** Work a first row of stitches going from left to right (clockwise on curves) and inserting needle downward. Alternate long and short stitches.

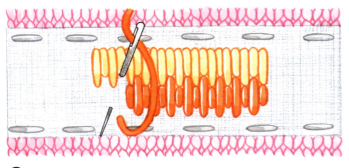

**2** Work second row from right to left, alternating long and short stitches and reversing positions from previous row.

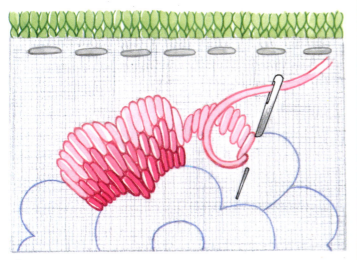

**3** If the motif is particularly complex, you can work rows in graduating shades of color (e.g., from light pink to dark pink). If the design allows, you can make alternating long and short points converge at motif center.

### Couched Stitch

Use needlework canvas (see page 131), unless embroidery is small or very easy.

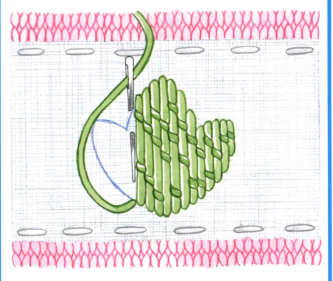

**1** Work from right to left, making a vertical stitch the length of design (as shown). Bring needle out a short distance below the entry point.

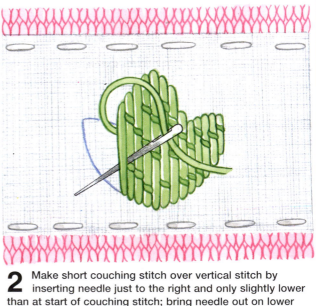

**2** Make short couching stitch over vertical stitch by inserting needle just to the right and only slightly lower than at start of couching stitch; bring needle out on lower right for next couching stitch to left of vertical stitch. (Illustration shows correct position bringing needle out.)

Continue making long vertical stitches and couching them until design area is completed.

# motifs to embroider 1

**W**ith a little bit of imagi-
nation, you can transform
the appearance of a
sweater or other knitted
garment. Add a simple
figure embroidered in
duplicate stitch or cross
stitch, for example, sur-
rounded by small delicate
beads.

### ■ embroidering the alphabets

Choose the monogram desired and determine its position on
the garment. Then embroider it in duplicate stitch or cross
stitch. Following the chart, note that each square on chart
represents 1 knitted stitch in width and 2 rows in length.

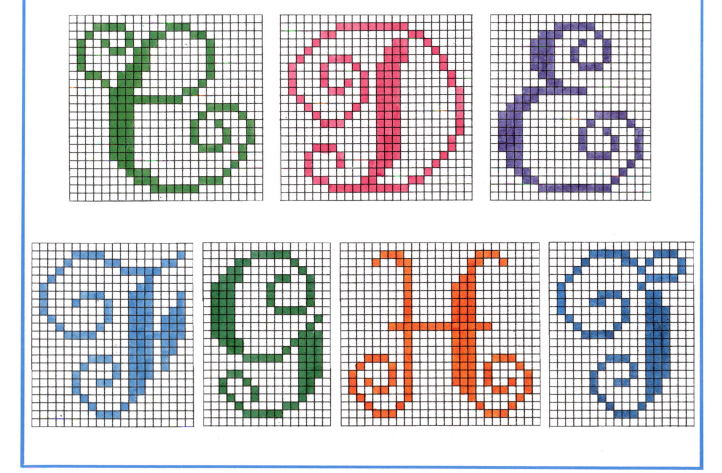

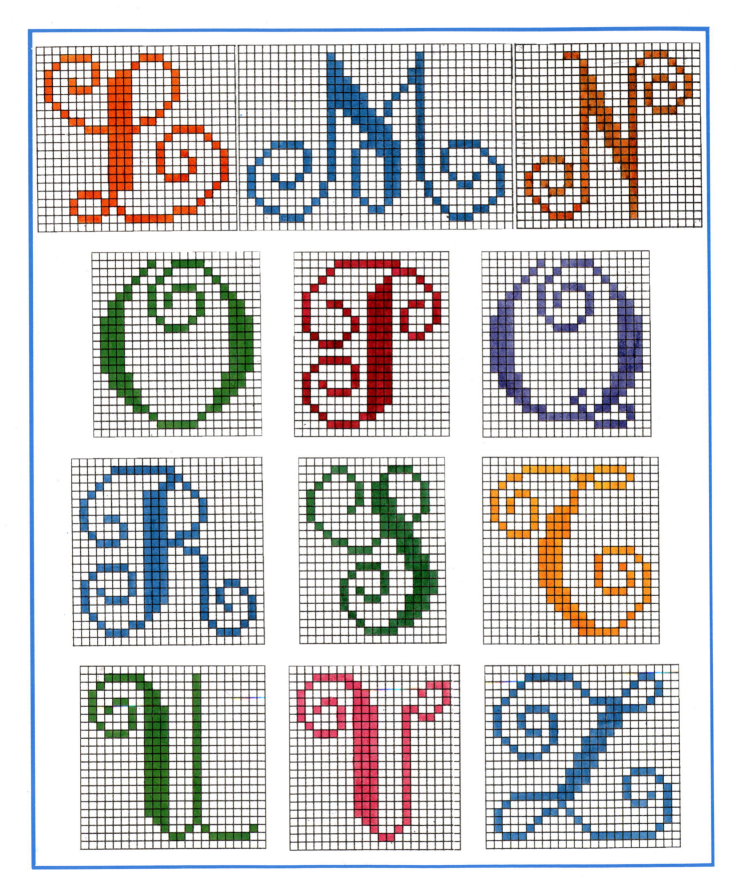

# motifs to embroider 2

### zodiac signs

Choose the zodiac sign desired and determine its position on the garment. Embroider it in duplicate stitch or cross stitch, following the chart. Note that each square on the chart represents 1 knitted stitch in width and 2 rows in length.

Aries

Taurus

Gemini

Cancer

Leo

Virgo

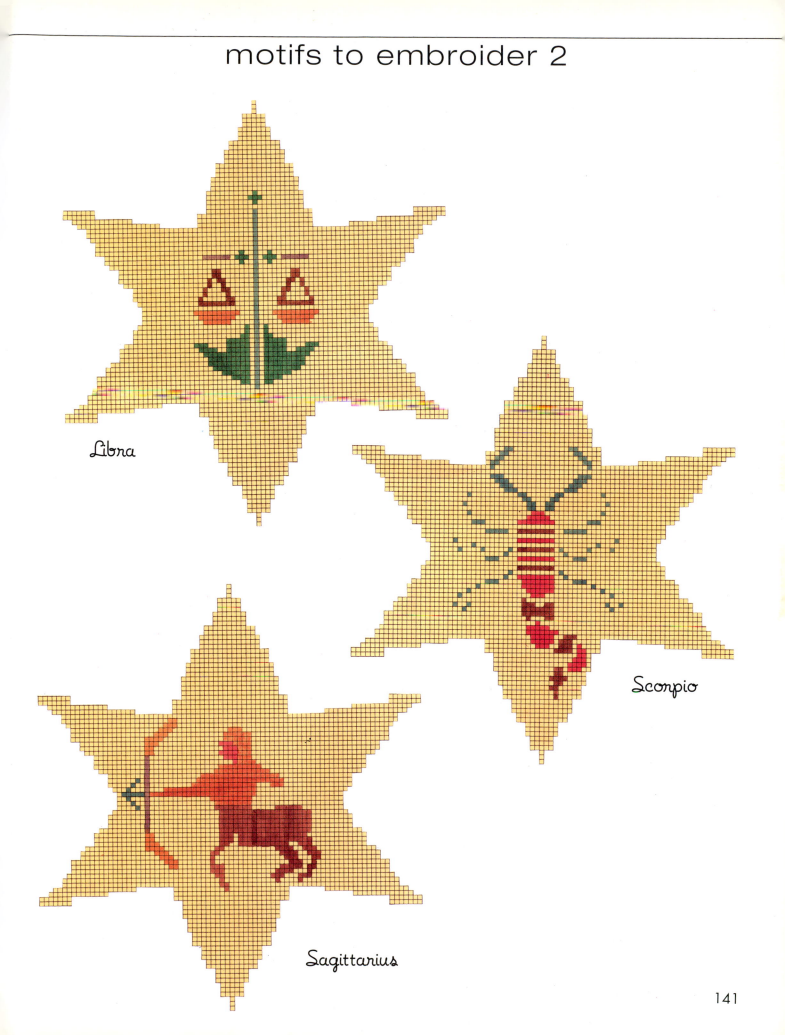

Libra

Scorpio

Sagittarius

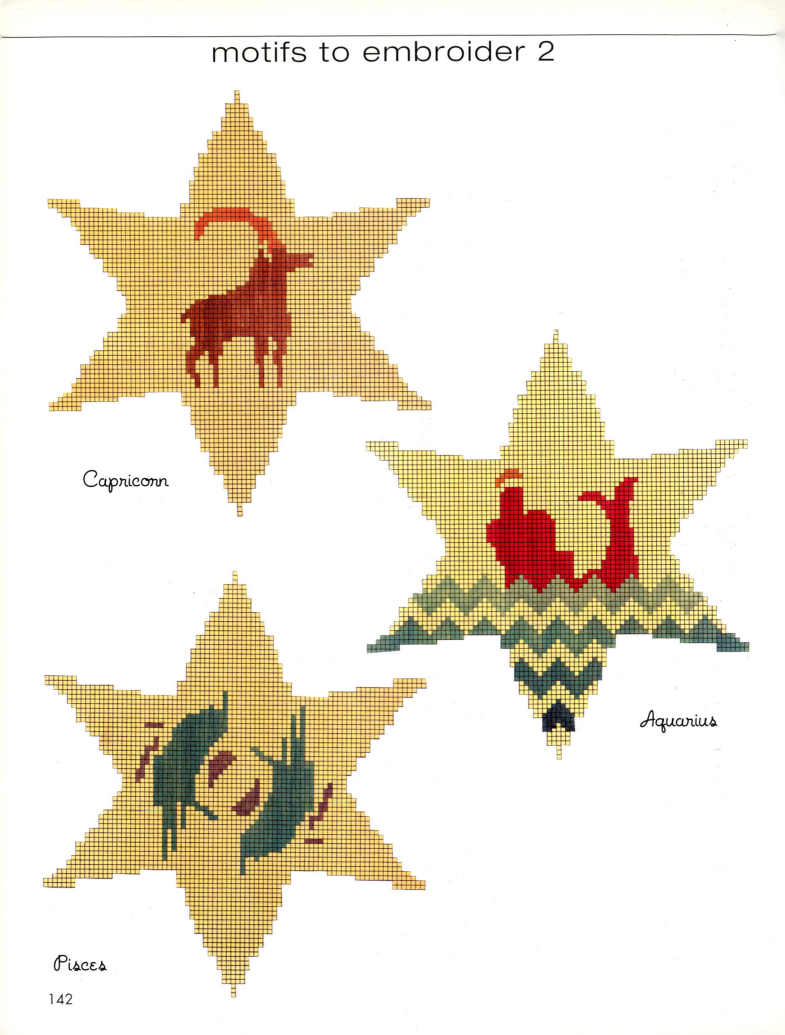

Capricorn

Aquarius

Pisces

142

# index

# index